Praise for *Get Better*

"A toolbox full of wisdom, an urgent starting point in finding possibility, potential, and power in the people around you."

—Seth Godin, author of *Linchpin*

"If you want to learn how to boost your emotional health and significantly strengthen your relationships at work, *Get Better* is a must read. This highly engaging book from my friend Todd Davis highlights fifteen proven practices that help you shift your thoughts and behaviors to optimize your effectiveness, relationships, and overall health."

—Dr. Daniel Amen, Director of the Amen Clinics and
ten-time *New York Times* bestselling author

"Relationships are a crucial element to a healthy and vibrant life. *Get Better* presents fifteen transformative practices that will bring a higher level of health and strength to your personal and professional relationships."

—Jillian Michaels, wellness expert, entrepreneur, and
eight-time *New York Times* bestselling author

"Everyone wants to get better and be better. It's a feeling and a notion without a roadmap or GPS. Now, at last, full disclosure on how you can get better, be better, do better, and fulfill your destiny. Enjoy reading, absorbing, and using the wisdom of Todd's book."

—Mark Victor Hansen

"*Get Better* will help you do just that—get better in all of your relationships— at work, at home, and in your community. A must read for anyone looking to improve how they 'relate' to others."

—Larry King

"This is a wonderful, insightful book, full of great ideas that can change your life and release your potential."

—Brian Tracy, author of
No Excuses!: The Power of Self-Discipline

"If you want to win at work, succeed at home, and live a happy and fulfilled life, relationships are key. In *Get Better,* Todd humbly shares his life experiences, along with the principles, practices, and patterns necessary for improving our daily associations with those who matter most and who have the greatest influence in our lives. *Get Better* is the best 'relationship read' of the year!"

—Michael Hyatt, *New York Times* bestselling author of *Your Best Year Ever*

"I have always believed that the workplace can only improve through the strengthening of relationships between people. In *Get Better,* we learn how to make these relationships meaningful and sustainable. If you believe that people are the key to business growth, *Get Better* will provide you with ways to unlock the potential of people and to create high-performing teams."

—Kimo Kippen, chief learning officer, Hilton Worldwide

GET
15 PROVEN PRACTICES TO BUILD EFFECTIVE RELATIONSHIPS AT WORK
BETTER

TODD DAVIS

Simon & Schuster Paperbacks

NEW YORK   LONDON   TORONTO   SYDNEY   NEW DELHI

Simon & Schuster Paperbacks
An Imprint of Simon & Schuster, Inc.
1230 Avenue of the Americas
New York, NY 10020

First Simon & Schuster trade paperback edition January 2019

SIMON & SCHUSTER PAPERBACKS and colophon are registered trademarks
of Simon & Schuster, Inc.

For information about special discounts for bulk purchases, please contact
Simon & Schuster Special Sales at 1-866-506-1949
or business@simonandschuster.com.

The Simon & Schuster Speakers Bureau can bring authors to your
live event. For more information or to book an event, contact the
Simon & Schuster Speakers Bureau at 1-866-248-3049
or visit our website at www.simonspeakers.com.

Cover and interior design by The Creative Lab at FranklinCovey

Manufactured in the United States of America

10 9 8 7 6 5 4 3 2 1

Library of Congress Cataloging-in-Publication Data is available.

ISBN 978-1-5011-5830-8
ISBN 978-1-5011-5831-5 (pbk)
ISBN 978-1-5011-5832-2 (ebook)

CONTENTS

FOREWORD

Bob Whitman
Chairman and CEO

FranklinCovey is a global company specializing in performance improvement. We help organizations achieve results that require a change in human behavior. So how easy is it to change behavior? Just think about how difficult it can be to change your own attitudes and behavior, let alone changing the behavior of someone else, or lots of someone elses!

In authoring *Get Better: 15 Practices to Build Effective Relationships at Work*, Todd Davis makes the compelling case that the key to improving our effectiveness, relationships, and results is to begin *getting better* ourselves by focusing first on improving our own paradigms and behaviors. As we do, we increase our ability to influence those around us for good, starting with the important relationships in our personal and professional lives.

Why put a priority on strengthening our effectiveness in building our key relationships? Because the strength of our relationships is the foundation for the culture we establish in both our work and in our personal lives. This culture, in turn, drives everything else. Everything gets better, becomes more effective, and is more meaningful when our key relationships, both at work and in our private lives, are rich and effective.

Think about it. Without excellent customer relationships, what happens to your business? Everything slows down or stops. Without excellent employee relationships, what happens? Battles break out and productivity implodes. Without excellent personal relationships, what happens? Your entire life is less happy and fulfilling.

Most organizations state, "People are our greatest asset." While he believes firmly that people are indeed any organization's most important asset, Todd takes us beyond this discussion when he suggests that "it's not only people, but the nature of *relationships* between and among people that truly establishes our competitive advantage."

It's true. Over the past decade, Franklin Covey has studied the outcomes achieved by the tens of thousands of operating units in thousands of companies. One study revealed that the factors which accounted for the biggest differences between the results achieved by the highest-performing units and those achieved by their lesser-performing counterparts was fundamentally the quality of their relationships with both customers and employees. Those units having the best and most effective relationships with their customers and employees, as measured by customer loyalty and employee-engagement levels, significantly outperformed those units with just average customer-employee relationships.

FranklinCovey was founded decades ago on the premise that great organizations are built on the foundation of great relationships with all key stakeholders. Beginning with the publication of the award-winning *The 7 Habits of Highly Effective People*, and continuing with the best-selling *The Speed of Trust, The 4 Disciplines of Execution,* and *The 5 Choices to Extraordinary Productivity,* the company has focused on unleashing human potential through world-class content, insights, and training. You will find FranklinCovey's works on the bookshelves of corporate leaders in every country on every continent.

Todd Davis has a deep well of wisdom on the topic of relationships. As the longtime chief people officer at FranklinCovey, a company that specializes in achieving lasting behavioral change, he's a unique guide to have on the subjects of relationships and continuous improvement. He is a vital spokesman on the topic of those universal principles of human and organizational effectiveness we stand for; beyond that, he is a living, breathing example of how to *practice* those principles.

In this book, Todd describes some of the most common stumbling blocks over which many of us trip at one time or another: blaming others for our problems, focusing on the urgent but not important things, jumping to a solution before we even understand the problem, and so forth. In his wisdom, he also provides simple but practical ways to avoid those relationship stumbling blocks and *get better* at whatever we do.

In so many ways, Todd has demonstrated that the strength of our relationships is our most important asset, and that our relationships with each other are not only the *means to* our success but also the most enduring *reward for* our success.

One of FranklinCovey's most important objectives and values is to become the workplace of choice for achievers with heart. As CEO, I have depended on Todd's wisdom and experience to attract and retain the best talent to be found. I have marveled at his sensitivity as a counselor and coach to our thousands of employees.

Listening to—and now reading—Todd's wisdom has been of inestimable value and joy to me. I'm confident it will be to you as well.

INTRODUCTION

One of the famous (if slightly erroneous) conclusions from the philosopher Jean-Paul Sartre's play *No Exit* is that "hell is other people."[1] The premise is that three souls find themselves in the afterlife—comprised of a single room with no doors or mirrors—and come to realize that not only are they stuck there forever, but they happen to really irritate the you-know-what out of each other. If you've ever been stuck in a middle seat on a full flight, you may have experienced something similar. Sartre found relationships so pivotal to one's happiness that, when they go bad, it can literally feel like hell. I've heard similar sentiments over the years as I've served as the chief people officer for one of the most people-centric organizations in the world. When people feel disconnected, disenfranchised, or disillusioned at work, such feelings tend to be tied to those with whom they work: their boss, team members, colleagues, and even direct reports. As a result, I've written this book around a simple but powerful premise: At the heart of what makes us fulfilled and effective, both in our personal and our professional lives, is the quality of our relationships.

There is evidence to support just how important the quality of our relationships is. Take the findings of the Harvard Grant Study, in which researcher Dr. Robert Waldinger reported, "People who are more isolated than they want to be from others find that they are less happy, their health declines earlier in midlife, their brain functioning declines sooner, and they live shorter lives. . . ."[2] Or recently Google's in-depth analysis that found high-quality relationships were at the heart of highly successful teams.[3]

You've probably heard the adage that an organization's greatest assets are its people. I'd like to take that one step further and share that, in my experience, it's the *relationships* between those people that create the culture and, in the end, become an organization's ultimate competitive advantage. In other words, at both the individual and organizational levels, relationships matter; nearly everything gets better when we focus on strengthening them. But there are old habits and biases standing in the way. When we find ourselves stuck in Sartre's metaphorical room, surrounded by people we disagree with or who simply rub us the wrong way, often our first instinct is to point the finger at *them*. It's their fault: If only my boss understood me better, or my colleagues respected me more, or my partner would listen. This is Sartre's hell, where we stay awash in our victimhood and, rather than take responsibility for ourselves, denigrate and blame everyone else. And if we don't just give up and consign ourselves to our fate, often the next instinct is to find a way out. This might mean leaving a team, a company, or even a marriage. There's a strong temptation to look for an external change to make things right again. After all, a new and better room (with more reasonable people) lies just beyond the next door! But what happens when we arrive? Often we find ourselves in a new room with new people—inherently flawed as all humans are—with whom we must now learn to get along. We are simply the same person traversing one room to the next, carrying with us the same limiting beliefs that keep us ever stuck without an exit. And yes, it can feel like hell.

There is a way out.

It begins, as most things do, with a new way of thinking. As one of the senior leaders responsible for our culture at FranklinCovey, I've had the unique opportunity to experience this firsthand. In many organizations, my role oversees benefits, payroll, compliance, training, and other traditional HR functions—things that happen *to* people. And while those are important, we make a more meaningful contribution when we address what takes place *between* people—when we get better at understanding and improving the nature of our relationships. That is the "people part" of the chief people officer title.

When I first moved into the role, I certainly had a strong sense that nothing slowed work down more than problematic relationships. As time went on, experience after experience validated what I initially suspected: that effective relationships yield effective results. I've learned that nothing of significance happens without a focus on improving our interactions with one another. And while the natural tendency is to focus on what we want to "fix" in others, the best results come when we first start with ourselves. To quote the late Dr. Stephen R. Covey, author of the best-selling book *The 7 Habits of Highly Effective People*, cofounder of FranklinCovey, and recognized by *Time* magazine as one of the twenty-five most influential Americans, "All meaningful change comes from the inside out."

While I don't claim to be the originator of the many principles and paradigms that have come from this great firm, I have had the opportunity to see them in action, witnessing both the benefits when they were practiced and the costs when they were ignored. To this end, I present this book as a series of conversations and experiences I've had (or that have been shared with me from clients and others around the world) over the course of twenty-plus years. And while I've changed certain details to protect the privacy of those involved, these are the stories I felt most compelled to tell—stories of how our paradigms come to shape how we experience and interact with the world, of relationships saved and lost, of careers stunted or accelerated, and of those unique individuals who have helped me and many others in our organization get better at practically everything we do. While I have a deep well of lessons learned from failure, I've drawn mostly from examples of positive conversations over my life to illustrate the power of these practices. It is from such intersections of the theoretical and the practical that I have experienced my most profound and meaningful insights.

There are numerous practices that affect relationships, but I've chosen to write about fifteen that, in my experience, make the most significant impact. I'll discuss why not living them can feel like Sartre's hell, and prompt you with a question at the beginning of each chapter designed to help you surface your own experiences around that practice. You'll also find most of the practices start with a story that doesn't conclude until the end of the chapter. These bookends help frame the practice by illustrating where people typically get stuck and their resolutions. Each time I reintroduce the story at the end, I purposefully repeat a portion of the story to remind you of the original situation.

You can read this book from front to back, or you can scan the question at the beginning of each practice to identify a timely or deeply felt relationship challenge, and read that one first. And the "Get Better" applications at the end of each practice allow you to put a specific practice to work in your own life, if you choose. What's most important, however, is that you approach this book with an open heart and mind, and consider the possibility that the only way to truly get better with others is to begin with yourself. It's been my experience that, by doing so, it will pay benefits in practically every area of your life.

GET
BETTER

WEAR GLASSES THAT WORK

> **HAVE YOU EVER DISCOVERED THAT YOUR VERSION OF THE SUPPOSED TRUTH WASN'T SO TRUE OR COMPLETE AFTER ALL?**

If so, you may want to consider

PRACTICE 1: WEAR GLASSES THAT WORK.

If you don't wear glasses that work, your "room" may feel like Sartre's hell because:

- You act on incorrect information.
- You don't get the results you want.
- You feel foolish when you recognize your version of the truth is limited and inaccurate.

Jon walked into my office, sharply dressed and with an air of urgency. He ran a team that constantly felt the pressure to hit aggressive quality and deadline goals, and had a reputation for being frustrated with anyone or anything that slowed things down. I could read his expression at once: he wasn't happy.

"Todd, you have a moment?" he asked as he walked in and shut the door behind him. He knew full well I had an open-door policy as the chief people officer, especially when my door was open.

"Sure," I replied, inviting him to take a seat. He hesitated, likely resisting the urge to pace back and forth while he talked. He nodded and sat down, looking uncomfortable at the sudden lack of motion.

"So what's going on?" I prompted. Jon rubbed his eyes and gathered his thoughts.

"It's Isabel," he said, obviously frustrated. "She's dragging her feet and putting the deadline at risk—again." Isabel was a project manager and Jon's peer. Thoughtful, intelligent, and a big-picture thinker, she was a valuable and trusted member of the organization. She also seemed immune to Jon's sense of urgency.

"I see. How can I be of help?"

"I need someone like you to reason with her," Jon replied. "I'm not a people person."

● ● ●

Jon's declaration that he wasn't a "people person" reminded me that we view not only ourselves, but those around us, through a set of lenses; and like any lens, they either sharpen or distort reality. I use this metaphor purposefully, as it was something I experienced when I learned my vision needed correcting. I remember putting on that first pair of glasses in second grade and being surprised by what I discovered: For the first time, I could see the leaves on the trees a few blocks away! Myriad other details that had gone unnoticed were suddenly visible, and my entire world took on a vibrant clarity.

The funny thing is, until that point, I had no idea what I was missing. To me, everything looked just as it should and it all made sense. No wonder my art teacher recommended a career in accounting! It took a new pair of glasses to see just how much I hadn't noticed. You might think that finding a few extra leaves is trivial in the larger scheme of things, but there's a greater truth at work. As philosopher and author Thomas Kuhn wrote, "All significant breakthroughs are break-withs old ways of thinking."[4] As it turns out, what we see informs how we think and feel, which influences what we do and the results we ultimately get.

Years ago a good friend of mine decided to get in shape and start running. This decision was important to him for several reasons, including a desire to live a healthier life and have increased energy to spend with his family. He did well for the first two days, but on the third, he tripped on a crack in the pavement and sprained his ankle. It was a painful injury that sidelined his efforts and required several months to heal.

When the time came to trade in his crutches for running shoes, he didn't do it. He decided to give up on running altogether, despite how important it had been to his goal of realizing a healthy lifestyle. My friend put on a particular set of glasses, seeing himself as not athletic and the world as full of pitfalls. This view influenced his thoughts (that he'd made a mistake trying to run in the first place); those thoughts influenced his feelings (he was unmotivated and fearful); and those feelings drove his behavior (he ended up back on the couch). The goals that had been so important to him were forgotten.

How we view ourselves and the world around us is called a paradigm. This term has become so commonplace that, chances are, you've played "buzzword bingo" during an office meeting, and "Paradigm Shift" was one of the options. To quote Dr. Covey:

IF YOU WANT TO MAKE MINOR CHANGES IN YOUR LIFE, WORK ON YOUR BEHAVIOR. IF YOU WANT SIGNIFICANT, QUANTUM BREAKTHROUGHS, WORK ON YOUR PARADIGMS.

Let's return to my friend and take a closer look at what was really going on. His ankle had healed, he had two normally functioning legs, and he was in good (but not great) health. His doctor told him he could—and probably should—take up running again, and that new pair of shoes was just sitting in the closet waiting to be laced up. And yes, the world is full of cracks in the pavement, but he can be on the lookout and learn to navigate them better. Imagine if my friend were to swap his limiting lenses for something more helpful:

- **Seeing.** I am physically able to run and navigate the small obstacles that come my way.
- **Thinking.** I can and should take up running again.
- **Feeling.** I'm optimistic I can reach the goals that are important to me.
- **Doing.** I'm pulling the shoes out of the closet and going for a run!

Simply choosing how we see ourselves and others has a cascading effect on what we think, feel, and do. This concept is a foundational principle for making significant changes in our lives. Consider some of the common ways we may inaccurately view ourselves and others:

- I don't belong.
- I'm too lazy.
- I'm impatient.
- I'll never be good enough.
- I can't change—I am what I am.

We also have some common ways in which we may inaccurately view the world or others:

- Everything is against me.
- Things usually turn out bad.
- My friend is thoughtless.
- My colleague doesn't know what he's doing.

- People can't be trusted.
- My team will never change.

Running was the basis for one of my own struggles with this principle, and it had a profound impact on me and one of the relationships that mattered most in my life. By the way, my preference for running stories reminds me of the old joke: How do you know if someone runs a marathon? Don't worry, they'll tell you!

Years ago my daughter, Sydney, like many teenagers, had her share of struggles with self-esteem. Compounding this struggle was the fact she had lost her hearing at an early age. It often made it difficult for her to communicate and served as fodder for the kind of teasing such challenges incite. I had recently taken up running, and wondered if completing a marathon might be good for her. She seemed to like the idea, so we started training together. Before long, however, she began to struggle. Between the early mornings and constant grind, it ended up being too much for her, and she dropped out. I was disappointed at first, but to be honest, I was also a little relieved that I could focus on my own goal of finishing the marathon in under four hours.

The race came and went. I didn't make my goal and Sydney continued to have life struggles.

The next year I asked if she'd like to give it another shot. She agreed and we were back at it. Sydney hung in a little longer this time; but eventually, the mornings grew colder, her muscles grew sore, and she quit again. Again, I was disappointed, but I went back to my own training regimen. The race came and went. I didn't make my goal, and Sydney continued to have struggles.

The following year I paused and reevaluated what was going on. Obviously, my good intentions weren't working. I carefully thought about my daughter and how truly strong she was. I had seen her overcome barriers related to her hearing loss that I couldn't imagine taking on. She had an almost unbelievable combination of strength and resilience. And if that were true—and I knew it was—the problem didn't rest with her. I realized that I had never really seen her as being capable of completing the marathon. This belief expressed itself in the way we trained in the previous two attempts. For instance (I'm almost embarrassed to admit it), because she ran slower, I would often run around her so I could focus on my own conditioning. I was actually *running around her*! I can't even imagine how discouraging it must have been having someone literally run circles around you every morning during your training. I'm sure Sydney thought she was holding me back, and that made it even easier for her to quit.

When I asked Sydney to run the marathon the third time, I expressed how I absolutely knew she could do it. And this time, I believed it! Therefore, so did she. We started training again, but now I focused completely on her. Sometimes it would materialize as little things, like me carrying the water bottles for both of us so she could concentrate on her form. Or in bigger things, like running slightly behind her so that she pushed her pace. This time Sydney didn't quit; and that, in and of itself, was a great achievement. I knew there was more: I saw my daughter as someone who had the strength to not only make it to the starting line, but to the finish line as well.

Race day came, and I knew Sydney was going to finish. My only concern at this point was making sure we finished before they took down the balloons and ended all of the hoopla at the finish line. Based on our final training runs, I suspected we would come in around the five-and-a-half-hour mark . . . maybe five hours and twenty minutes if we really pushed it.

The race began and we took off. At about mile sixteen, I actually remember telling Sydney that the race was going by too fast. She looked at me like I was crazy. What sane person running a marathon ever complains of it going by too fast? But that was my feeling, because I was so enjoying watching Sydney accomplish this amazing goal. We crossed the finish line long before the balloons came down with a time of four hours and twenty-three minutes. We were exuberant, and she was on top of the world. It was a moment I will never forget. Crossing the finish line of my first marathon was thrilling, but nothing could compare to being with my daughter in this moment as she crossed *her* first finish line. And to think it might not have ever happened had I continued to see Sydney through the wrong glasses.

Here's how the "Wear Glasses That Work" pattern played out for me when it came to my daughter:

- **Seeing.** I chose to see Sydney as someone with the strength and capability to finish a marathon.
- **Thinking.** I changed my conditioning strategy from focusing on both of us to focusing on just her.
- **Feeling.** I had confidence in her and what she could do—confidence I knew she felt.
- **Doing.** We trained in such a way that we both crossed the finish line together.

Whenever I contemplate this topic, I'm reminded of the words purportedly carved on an Anglican bishop's tombstone in Westminster Abbey:

WHEN I WAS YOUNG AND FREE AND MY IMAGINATION HAD NO LIMITS, I DREAMED OF CHANGING THE WORLD.

AS I GREW OLDER AND WISER, I DISCOVERED THE WORLD WOULD NOT CHANGE, SO I SHORTENED MY SIGHTS SOMEWHAT AND DECIDED TO CHANGE ONLY MY COUNTRY.

BUT IT, TOO, SEEMED IMMOVABLE.

AS I GREW INTO MY TWILIGHT YEARS, IN ONE LAST DESPERATE ATTEMPT, I SETTLED FOR CHANGING ONLY MY FAMILY, THOSE CLOSEST TO ME, BUT ALAS, THEY WOULD HAVE NONE OF IT.

AND NOW, AS I LIE ON MY DEATHBED, I SUDDENLY REALIZE: IF I HAD ONLY CHANGED MYSELF FIRST, THEN BY EXAMPLE I WOULD HAVE CHANGED MY FAMILY. FROM THEIR INSPIRATION AND ENCOURAGEMENT, I WOULD THEN HAVE BEEN ABLE TO BETTER MY COUNTRY, AND WHO KNOWS, I MAY HAVE EVEN CHANGED THE WORLD.

We do a great disservice to ourselves when we wear the limiting lenses that are so often a part of human nature. But the good news is that changing one's glasses is a choice, and we all have the power to do so—even my colleague Jon.

• • •

"I need someone like you to reason with her," Jon replied. "I'm not a people person."

And there it was—the all-too-common view that we are simply who we are and we can't change. I knew Jon came into my office looking to recruit me as an ally to influence Isabel, but I felt there was something more important going on. "Jon, tell me why you believe that?"

"Believe what?"

"That you're not a people person."

I could tell from his expression that it wasn't the response he had anticipated. He cleared his throat before continuing. "Well, you know how it is."

I pressed on. "How is it, exactly?"

Jon sighed. "Look, I'm a results guy." This script was a well-worn groove I'd heard countless times before. (For those of you born after 1980, google "record player" for more information on how all this "groove" business works.) "I push, I get results and, by doing so, I sometimes turn people off. I'm just not good at the soft stuff."

"Remind me, you've been married how many years now?" I asked, knowing full well what the answer was.

"Nineteen."

I knew that Jon was both an amazing husband and father, so I wasn't buying in to his current view of himself. "Sounds like you've got a handle on some of that soft stuff after all."

Jon opened his mouth to object but stopped himself. I think he knew me well enough to realize I wasn't about to let this go. Instead, he raised his hands and slumped back into the chair. "Fine, I surrender."

"Let's say that you really are a people person then," I continued, "how would you handle the situation with Isabel?"

"Well, I suppose I should be talking with her instead of you."

I nodded. "I like how you said talking, because it's about mutual respect and a shared purpose. I imagine you and Isabel both want the same things. So my suggestion is that you reject the notion that you're not a people person and go and have a constructive conversation with your colleague. You might also want to consider the paradigm you have about Isabel."

"What do you mean?"

"Well, I have a hard time believing Isabel isn't as equally concerned about meeting the deadline."

Jon thought it over. "Yeah, I'll think about that. Good point."

As Jon got out of his seat, he looked like he was doing his best to hold back a smile. "You really enjoy this 'people' stuff, don't you?"

WEAR GLASSES THAT WORK

Take a moment to evaluate the glasses you're currently wearing and if you should exchange them for ones that work better. Use this exercise to help determine if you're wearing the right glasses.

1. Identify a relationship that feels off or challenging.

2. Like the example in the table below, list the reasons you think it's not working.

3. On the list you've created, underline which reasons are facts—things about which most people would agree.

4. Any remaining items are likely opinions or paradigms you have about the person that may be incomplete. Consider each one carefully, then ask yourself: Are any of my opinions worth reconsidering? Which opinions (that I formerly thought of as "facts") might I change? What would be the outcome if I changed them?

5. Draft a more complete paradigm worth considering.

6. Identify which actions you will take, based on glasses that work.

REASONS	NEW PARADIGM (GLASSES THAT WORK)	ACTIONS
Marietta is always defensive and alienates others. She acts like she knows more than she does. *She is one of the highest performers on the team. She graduated at the top of her class.* But she is insecure and trying to make up for it by becoming an authority on everything.	Marietta wants to do a good job and means well. She may need more encouragement from me and more experience to learn how to collaborate with others.	I will schedule a meeting with Marietta to better understand her, to share specific feedback about the good work she is doing, and to coach her on how to better engage with others.

CARRY YOUR OWN WEATHER

DO YOU EVER FIND THAT YOU'RE CONTROLLED BY OTHER PEOPLE, CIRCUMSTANCES, OR YOUR OWN KNEE-JERK REACTIONS?

If so, you may want to consider

PRACTICE 2: CARRY YOUR OWN WEATHER.

When you don't carry your own weather, your room may feel like Sartre's hell because:

- Life happens *to* you.
- Being a martyr becomes your brand.
- You limit your ability to positively influence others.

"Have you ever had to fire someone who was a favorite of everyone in the company?"

The question caught me off guard. I put my soda down and considered the man sitting across from me. We'd done some work together over the years and had kept a cordial relationship, which usually amounted to catching up over lunch when he was in town.

"I'm wondering if there's a question behind the question," I posed. My friend nodded, and I noticed a kind of weariness about him.

"Yesterday I spent hours meeting with the co-workers of a guy I had to fire. Everyone was really upset. Honestly, I was too—I can't count the number of times I've gone out of my way to help him."

I knew there could be several reasons to let someone go, and the last thing I wanted to do was pry into personal details, but obviously, my friend had something on his mind.

"I've had to let people go myself," I replied sympathetically. "It's never easy."

My friend nodded. "He really touched a nerve with me. I mean, I've done a lot for this guy. And it's not like he embezzled money or anything, but in a way, that makes the betrayal even worse."

"Worse? What do you mean?"

"Turns out he was doing work for a competing organization after hours, and he never mentioned it. It shows you how little he thinks of me and the company that's supported him," he replied, growing angry. "I can't believe he traded it all for practically nothing."

"So how did it turn from a discussion to a firing?"

"Well, there wasn't really much of a discussion. When I found out what had been going on, I let him go. Now, even the CEO is questioning my decision, and everyone thinks I'm the bad guy in all of this."

I had to hide my growing concern—maybe the CEO hadn't been that far off. Then again, there was probably more to the story.

"Look, loyalty matters to me, and people know that I make decisions quickly," my friend continued. "I had no choice."

● ● ●

I believe we are never without choice. Of course, that doesn't mean things don't happen outside of our control, or that our choices can't be severely limited. As immortalized in the words of Viktor Frankl, Holocaust survivor and author of *Man's Search for Meaning*: "Everything can be taken from a man but one thing: the last of the human freedoms—to choose one's attitude in any given set of circumstances, to choose one's own way."[5]

I have a colleague who shared the story of a memorable professor he'd had as an undergrad. Every day, this short and somewhat rotund man would walk across the college campus, coffee in hand, seemingly incapable of being in anything but a good mood. He would greet students warmly, often stopping to talk with them about their day and was one of the most popular professors on campus. One morning a spring thunderstorm broke over the school and, having misplaced his umbrella, the professor still took his usual walk to class. When he arrived, he remained as cheerful as ever as the students peeled off their various layers of wet gear, somewhat annoyed at the unexpected downpour. One student, noticing the professor's ever-pleasant disposition but soaked shirt, remarked, "Hey, Chuck, aren't you at all bothered by the rain?" Chuck smiled in response.

"Sure, but I benefit from my lack of height—it takes longer for the rain to reach me."

Not a single person on the campus had any control over the weather. Most reacted to the unwelcomed moisture by allowing their moods or the external nature of the storm to negatively affect them. They complained about the sudden drop in temperature or the fact that they got a bit wet. They allowed the darkening clouds to dictate their mood, longing for the sun to make an appearance and lift their spirits. It's easy to feel like a victim with such thoughts, surrendering to the belief that we're helplessly subject to the external world. And when others are the source of our dismay and helplessness, it's easy to cast blame, level accusations, and adopt a victim mindset and language.

However, the professor made a different choice. Rather than react to the weather outside, he carried his own. He looked inward instead of outward. This happy teacher decided how he was going to think and feel based on what he valued, regardless of whatever storm happened to break. This choice is a defining characteristic between those who choose to carry their own weather and those who don't—reacting to the external world as a victim or staying true to what you ultimately value. In the case of our short-statured professor, he valued the opportunity to come to class and do what he loved, to create a positive environment where his students could learn, and to plant educational seeds that might bear fruit for years to come. What was a little rain compared to *that*?

The esteemed Bishop Fulton J. Sheen, well known for his early radio and television work, expressed it this way: "Each of us makes his own weather—determines the color of the skies in the emotional universe which he inhabits."

At the foundation of carrying your own weather is the ability to pause between stimulus and response. The earliest humans learned "fight or flight" as a way of reacting to potentially life-threatening situations. Fast-forward to the modern world. For most of us, the challenge of daily survival is no longer the standard. Our stresses now come in different, less life-threatening forms. Yet, external stimuli naturally cause us to react quickly, and sometimes inappropriately.

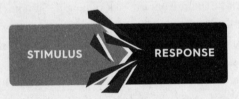

Thankfully, we have more than just the reactive part of our brain to work with. As human beings, we share the unique trait of self-awareness—the ability to see and evaluate our own thoughts. It gives us the capability to pause, step back, and see ourselves along with the paradigms we adopt and use. In effect, it gives us the freedom to proactively choose our response.

My good friend and colleague Aaron, who works as the director of recruitment in our organization, is an example of this principle. The best recruiters tend to put a lot of time and energy into finding and presenting the right person to the organization, and Aaron is no exception. I remember one candidate Aaron had worked with for several months. This highly sought-after individual was fielding overtures from several companies, but Aaron had gone to great lengths to build a relationship and favorably present our organization to her. I even remember Aaron going out of his way to meet with her on a Saturday, giving up his own free time with his family because it was the only day she could fly in. This person was truly exceptional. She stood out from all the other candidates presented to the team.

After all the time and energy Aaron had invested in the recruitment process and final interview, the hiring manager got back to him: "We really like her," the manager announced, "but we'd like you to look for a few more candidates we could interview."

Most people would want to put a fist through the wall at this point. Aaron knew this exceptional candidate would be recruited by another organization. I was there when the news was delivered and had been rooting for this candidate all along. I struggled with my own rush of emotions as I watched Aaron listen and draw a slow breath. Remarkably, he pushed the "pause button." "Sure, I understand," Aaron responded. "I know you need to have confidence that we've found the right person to succeed in this role. I'm happy to keep looking."

Frankly, I was amazed. My respect for Aaron deepened. Later, I pulled him aside and asked how he managed to be so positive in the face of this frustrating rejection. "Todd, if the hiring manager isn't excited about the candidate, that person isn't going to succeed," he replied. "And since that's the outcome that matters, I just need to find the right fit."

I wish I'd had Aaron's maturity earlier in my career.

As a young recruiter myself, I'd engaged a colleague to work with me, but it turned out she wouldn't come for less than a thousand dollars more than the company was paying me to do a similar job. To my surprise, my boss approved the higher salary request. I was incensed. "Wait a minute!" I complained. "I've been with the company for four years. I found this person, and now you're going to pay her more than you pay *me*?"

My boss simply responded that you pay what it takes to get the right person. I returned to my office full of negative and angry thoughts. *It's not fair! Why should I get paid less? My boss doesn't appreciate me. Maybe I should stop working so hard. Maybe I should look for a job somewhere else?* These thoughts persisted over the next few days, and I essentially wallowed in my own victimhood. One evening I was complaining about the situation to my dad, expounding on the great injustice I was suffering. He listened patiently as I blamed my boss, my friend, the job itself, and anything else I could come up with. When I had finished, he looked me in the eye and asked, "Have you thought about what *you* could do to qualify for the extra thousand dollars? Fairness in the marketplace is about getting a fair price for what you can do."

Suddenly, it hit me. I'd been spending my time reacting to my emotions rather than choosing to focus on what I could do to influence the situation. Where I saw a great and woeful injustice, my father saw an opportunity to broaden my thinking about my role. The next day, I approached my boss and asked, "I appreciate you listening to my frustration the past few days over this pay issue. What would you need to see from me to consider raising my pay as well?"

I remember his reaction to this day—as if he'd been waiting for that simple question all along. "I'm so glad you asked, Todd," he replied. "Right now, it's taking ten months on average to recruit a new physician. If we could shorten the recruitment cycle to six months, I'd feel great about looking at your compensation." I reluctantly let go of feeling like a victim and started focusing my time and energy on shortening the recruitment cycle. And it worked! It was a tough lesson, but I learned the benefits of carrying my own weather versus the consequences of playing the victim.

Let me return to my colleague Aaron. The power of carrying your own weather is so great that it can overcome even the most difficult storms we face. At forty-three, Aaron went in for a routine eye exam; Aaron's doctors discovered a brain tumor that had been growing for the last fifteen years. Instead of panicking or falling into despair, Aaron calmly made appointments and went through the process of getting the tumor evaluated and treated. It was benign but was causing swelling on his optic nerve, which affected his vision. If left untreated, the tumor could become life-threatening. The doctors scheduled an emergency surgery to remove the growth.

The day after surgery, I visited Aaron. I was impressed with his positive attitude. "They think the surgery went well," he announced from the hospital bed. "They'll run some scans in a few weeks, but I'm feeling optimistic." As the weeks passed, his health continued to improve. I couldn't help but wonder if his attitude was a significant factor.

Months after the procedure, he met with us at work just to express his thanks for our support. He began to get emotional, not for the severity of the situation or the pain and suffering he'd had to endure, but because of his appreciation for the important relationships in his life. "I'm sorry," he told us, "I'm just overcome with gratitude—for my life, my family, and for my friends here at work."

Aaron decided a long time ago not to let external factors dictate how he would feel, which allowed him to deal with everything from recruiting challenges to one of the most traumatic periods in his life. As I reflected upon Aaron's ability to carry his own weather, I was hoping to be able to share the benefits of carrying one's own weather with my friend who had reactively fired his long-term employee.

● ● ●

"So how did it turn from a discussion to a firing?"

"Well, there wasn't really much of a discussion. When I found out what had been going on, I let him go. Now the CEO is questioning my decision, and everyone thinks I'm the bad guy in all of this."

I had to hide my growing concern; maybe the CEO was right. Then again, there was probably more to the story.

"Look, loyalty matters to me, and people know that I make decisions quickly," my friend continued. "I had no choice."

"May I ask you a question?" I posed. My friend nodded. "What do you want your reputation or legacy to be as a leader?"

My friend paused. "I'm not sure what you're getting at."

"I was thinking that we could take a step back from the termination and look at the larger picture."

"Okay," my friend replied as he thought it over. "I want to be known as a person who gets things done."

"Good. How about when it comes to people?" I asked.

"Well, I want them to get on board and get things done with me."

"Sure, but how do you want them to feel about you as their leader?"

My friend answered right away, "I want them to respect me."

I let the words hang in the air for a moment before continuing. "I know it may sound obvious, but why do you want to be respected?"

My friend stared at me over the table. "Why do I want to be respected? Well, I'm their leader for a reason. I hope I have something to teach or offer them."

"So let's continue with that thought. Imagine your team has gathered at your retirement party and they're each sharing what they personally learned from you. What would you want to hear?"

My friend thought it over for a moment. "I'd like to hear that they were as loyal to me as I was to them—that I took the time to mentor them and make their lives better."

"Okay, and please don't be offended by this question," I said, "but think about how you just handled this last situation. Does it reflect how you want to be seen as a leader in that regard?"

My friend stared at me from across the table. "I guess it doesn't—I kind of lost my temper."

"It sounds like you reacted that way because you felt that this employee was being disloyal."

"At the time, yes."

"And now?"

"I don't know. Maybe I jumped to the wrong conclusion. I mean, I never really sat down and talked with him about it."

"Perhaps that's why you're troubled by it now. You let your first emotions get in the way of taking the time to understand the situation. You made a choice that likely didn't align with your values, which, if I heard you right, includes being a mentor and a positive influence in your employees' lives."

My friend paused and then asked, "So, what do I do now?"

"What happened is over. I don't know how things work in your company, but you may want to begin some damage control with your CEO," I suggested. "And as difficult as it can be when our emotions are high, remember in the future, you always have the choice to hit the 'pause button,' even if it means taking a five-minute break to gather your thoughts. Use the time to reflect on what's important to you, like your legacy, or what gets said at that retirement party down the road."

"I suppose that's something to think about," my friend admitted. "Either way, looks like I have some work to do." I agreed, hoping my friend would take the lesson to heart.

Carrying one's weather can express itself in many ways: from the simple choice to keep a pleasant or professional disposition, to not allowing the events around us to spin the needle of our moral compass. But at the heart of it is always a choice, and that power can never be surrendered unless we allow it.

CARRY YOUR OWN WEATHER

We can strengthen our relationships by practicing proactive behaviors. Think of a person or situation that causes you to feel somewhat irritated or reactive. Decide right now which of the following behaviors you will try the next time that situation occurs:

- Create a space between stimulus and response by counting to ten, going for a walk, or telling someone you need time to reflect before responding.

- Seek more understanding of the person or situation before reacting by saying something like, "This isn't making sense to me, so I imagine I'm missing something. Can you help me understand a little more?"

- With the intent of not sending it, write an email or a letter to the person who has triggered you. Let it sit overnight, then read it again and see if it accurately reflects how you feel now and what you value.

- Construct a do-over. Consider a past situation in which your reactivity had a negative impact. What did you do or say, and what was the outcome? Now imagine a better, more effective way to respond in the future. What would be the positive consequences of responding in this new way?

BEHAVE YOUR WAY TO CREDIBILITY

HAVE YOU EVER TRIED TO TALK YOUR WAY OUT OF A PROBLEM YOU'VE BEHAVED YOURSELF INTO?

If so, you may want to consider

PRACTICE 3: BEHAVE YOUR WAY TO CREDIBILITY.

When you don't behave your way to credibility, your room may feel like Sartre's hell because:

- You're frustrated that people judge you on your behavior, not your good intentions.
- You're irritated because you feel you must prove yourself to others.
- Over time, no one trusts you or has confidence in you.

My friend Chelsea recently had a flat tire while driving to work. After putting the spare on, she headed to the franchise of a well-known national chain. The mechanic there found a nail in the sidewall of the tire and stated that there was no way to fix the puncture if the tread was lower than nine millimeters. Chelsea was disheartened to hear that she might have to purchase a new tire, but the mechanic wasn't finished. He went on to point out that, since she drove an all-wheel-drive vehicle, all four tires would need to be replaced if just one was bad. He measured the depth of the tread on the punctured tire and glumly announced that it was seven millimeters, so there was no other choice but to purchase a new set. He tallied up the total (over a thousand dollars) and made an appointment for the next day.

On the drive home, Chelsea decided to call her brother-in-law, Mike, a former automotive-parts salesman. The last thing she wanted to do was spend a thousand dollars, but she certainly wasn't an expert when it came to tires. Mike gave her the name of a small shop he trusted but she'd never heard of. She called the mechanic on duty and learned that she could buy the same set of tires for two hundred dollars less than what was previously quoted to her. She was anxious to save money, but hesitant to use an unknown business. Based on Mike's recommendation, however, she ended up driving to the smaller shop to purchase the tires.

The mechanic there asked if he could look at the punctured tire. In Chelsea's mind, she'd already committed to buying an entire new set, but didn't see any harm in his examining the original tire. The mechanic measured, then remeasured the tire, telling her that the tread measured nine millimeters, not seven millimeters. He went on to advise her that she didn't need four new tires. Instead, he recommended that Chelsea see the service manager at the dealership where she originally bought the car. He suggested that she get the same tire, but have them shave the tread to match the other three.

This advice would certainly cost the mechanic the sale, but he seemed genuinely concerned with helping Chelsea find the least expensive solution to her problem. As a result, my friend took his advice and ended up saving nearly eight hundred dollars. She also called the original store to not only cancel the appointment but to express her disappointment.

• • •

As Chelsea related the events of her flat-tire story, I wondered about the reputation each shop had earned. Both mechanics were presented with the same problem, but one behaved in a way that severely damaged his credibility with my friend and everyone she told. By contrast, the second mechanic increased his credibility and likely earned some new clients in the process. He did this by showcasing three principles of behaving with credibility:

• Demonstrating character and competence
• Taking the long-term view
• Adapting to the situation at hand

DEMONSTRATING CHARACTER AND COMPETENCE

Without a high degree of character and competence, people aren't going to trust you. You might think of me as someone who's thoughtful and considerate (character), but you might have reservations when I offer to pack your parachute for your first skydiving lesson (competence). Chances are you'd probably want to know just how much experience and/or training I'd had in parachute packing (none). And despite my amiable disposition and positive attitude, you'd be right to find me lacking credibility. In the same way, you might be hesitant if you learned the person who *had* packed your parachute was just acquitted of a manslaughter charge on a technicality: The individual might have every parachute-packing certification around, but if you feel something about the packer's character is off, it will likely cause concern. Now, this example is obviously a bit extreme, but without high character and high competence, credibility can't flourish. Because of this, it's worth diving a little deeper into each.

Character

I learned a valuable lesson about character as a young manager early in my career. My job was to negotiate contracts with the doctors who worked with my company, a health-maintenance organization. One year we brought in a new group of physicians with unique requirements. It took several weeks for our team to write a contract that would meet their needs. This all happened before we had computers and electronic files—everything was done on a typewriter (a device now mostly seen in museums). In any case, these original typed pages were passed back and forth for ongoing revisions, edits, and suggestions from the various team members. After weeks of work, we reached the point where the contract was about to be finalized and signed . . . only it was missing!

No one could find it. Each person who was thought to have been the last one to review it pointed the finger at someone else. We searched for more than a week trying to locate the paperwork, but with no luck—all while the clock was ticking toward the date we needed to implement the new contract with the physician group.

As frustrating as it was, we had no choice but to painstakingly re-create the contract from scratch. While the writing went a little faster this time, a great deal of effort was wasted. We eventually completed the new contract, put it in place, and the relationship was established.

One evening about six months later, I was looking through my desk drawers for an old file. As I pulled out various documents, to my horror, I discovered the missing contract—it had been in my desk the entire time! I had accidentally paper-clipped it to the back of another document and stuck it in the wrong folder.

I thought carefully about what my next steps should be. The new contract was in place; everyone was over their frustration and had moved on. My first thought was to toss the contract in the trash and tell no one. The last thing I wanted was for anyone to know *I* was the guy who was the cause of the near disaster and all the wasted effort. I went home and slept on it. The next morning, however, I found myself walking over to my boss's office with the lost contract in hand.

While I'd like to think my decision to tell the truth was a result of my high-minded character, I was more likely, at that age, to be driven by the fear that somebody would eventually find out, and my attempt to conceal the truth would only make matters worse.

"You're going to want to kill me," I said reluctantly to my boss as I handed the missing document to him, "but look what I found in my desk!"

He took the document and then looked at me for a long time. I waited for the impending explosion of anger. Instead, he said, "I admire you, Todd. I think I would have just thrown it away." We both laughed as I told him the idea had crossed my mind.

His response that day taught me a valuable lesson: that character wasn't built on being infallible, but by behaving in a way that proved to others I could be trusted, even when no one was looking.

Character is such an important attribute, I've written an entire section about it. (See "Practice 15: Start With Humility.")

Competence

Many people think strong character can make up for lack of competence. I'm reminded of Craig, a colleague I used to work with: He was reliable, pleasant, and no one ever questioned his honesty or integrity. He always remembered everyone's birthday, was considerate of others, and remembered the key events of clients' personal lives. He put people first.

There came a point in his career where both Craig and Marta, a fellow team member, were working with the same client. The client decided to engage our company in partnering on an additional project, requiring more work from either Craig or Marta. While both employees had good character, Marta had paid more of a price to invest in her competence. She had taken several postgraduate courses that resulted in an increase in her business acumen, and had shadowed several of our top consultants over the years. It was apparent that she was in a continual state of learning and getting better at her profession. Ultimately, the client hired Marta over Craig, the highly personable colleague, knowing Marta had paid the price to thoroughly understand the business. Craig was disappointed and even felt that the decision wasn't fair. He allowed his frustration to fester and, as the cycle repeated with additional clients, he eventually left the organization. Craig had lost credibility because he allowed his competence to wane.

Increasing competence often requires that we step outside our comfort zone. A friend shared the story of Malee, who was shy both by nature and culture, and struggling to earn the approbation of her team leaders. She was a good person, but if she couldn't get past her crippling shyness, she wouldn't end up being a good fit for the team. A change in management presented Malee with a new boss, who made participation in team meetings a mandatory part of performance reviews. When Malee learned that she needed to participate and share thoughts of how to improve processes, she was petrified. She had no confidence that her ideas were worthy of being heard and, even worse, had never spoken up in front of anyone in her life! But wanting to get better, she courageously asked her team leader Lisa to mentor and guide her. She admitted to Lisa that she'd recently been asked to give a talk in front of a community group to which she belonged. These were people who knew and liked her, and the topic was one she understood well, yet she still declined. Malee worried that if she couldn't speak in front of friends in her community, how could she ever bring herself to speak up in front of co-workers?

Lisa encouraged Malee to share her suggestions one-on-one before the team meetings. Lisa would then share Malee's ideas in the team meeting without attributing them to her so that she could see how people reacted to her ideas. Malee agreed, and she began meeting with Lisa weekly.

After only a few meetings, Malee saw her co-workers respond positively to her ideas. This response gave her the courage to start slowly sharing them herself, increasing her communication competency week by week. With positive feedback from Lisa and fellow teammates, eventually, Malee built her confidence level. Many of her team members were surprised at the insightful suggestions Malee started to share. She became courageous enough to recommend that they eliminate what she viewed was a redundant step in one of the manufacturing processes. This humble woman was amazed when her teammates agreed with her. It was a big change and would need to be presented to the executive committee. Her teammates elected Malee to present the idea. At first, she said no, but after considerable coaching from Lisa, she practiced over and over, enlisting her teammates to give helpful feedback. Malee ended up delivering her suggestion to the executive team, who implemented it. The idea ended up saving the company $65,000 in one year, and much more later. Her newly acquired competence around publicly sharing her ideas, as difficult as it was for her to overcome her fears, ended up building high levels of trust and credibility across the entire organization.

TAKING THE LONG-TERM VIEW

Credibility isn't earned overnight. Taking the long-term view means you are willing to pay the price to earn it—regardless of the time and effort involved. When I first joined FranklinCovey's HR department, I looked for ways to make things more efficient and effective. I noticed early on that the CEO approved all hires—from part-time receptionists to senior leaders. I immediately thought, *Here's an area where I could free up the CEO's time and make the hiring process more efficient.*

I scheduled a meeting with the CEO to discuss what he would need to see in order to feel comfortable allowing me to make the hiring decisions for certain roles. His response surprised me. "I appreciate you asking," he said. "But it's working well for me to always approve the positions."

I had a sense there was more behind his decision. I left the meeting a bit perplexed: Why would the CEO choose to spend his valuable time approving all new hires?

I continued to implement the current traditional process. Every two weeks he and I would meet to review every new hire or replacement request. It was a time-intensive process. He'd ask, "Is there anyone else who could do this job that we currently employ?" Or "What do we lose if this particular job doesn't get done anymore?" Or "If we were going to redesign this department, would we hire the same positions again?" The questions went on and on, and I couldn't help but wonder if he didn't think I had the credibility to make these kinds of decisions. As time passed, I started seeing patterns in his questions. I began to anticipate them. Each time we met, I had more of his questions already addressed. This process continued for quite some time, with me presenting the information and asking at the end, "Have I missed anything?" Every once in a while, the CEO would ask something I hadn't covered; but usually, I had anticipated and addressed his concerns in advance. I started to feel his trust in me build.

It would have been easy for me to wallow in my frustration and feel resentment in having my own credibility challenged in such a way. But by taking the long-term view, I was able to learn from the CEO and build skills that enhanced my credibility. I discovered a lot about the critical thinking that should go into every hire a company makes. It also gave me the opportunity to learn the *why* behind what I had initially viewed as overinvolvement. Over time, I learned that the CEO was driven by a sincere compassion for people, not a desire to do my job. His rigorous process had come from a time in our company's history where the right hiring processes weren't in place, and a restructure had ended up negatively impacting many lives. The CEO cared so much for people that he didn't ever want to face that situation again. Taking the long-term view gave me the patience I needed to determine what was important to him and to increase my credibility with him over time. It also gave me the opportunity to evaluate and strengthen the entire recruitment and hiring process.

When it comes to building credibility, there's no escaping time. Transitory actions may build confidence in others, but trust only comes from seeing the consistency of such actions over time. If we don't take the long-term view, our credibility will suffer. As with Chelsea and her flat tire, the second mechanic traded a short-term gain (selling a new set of tires) for a longer-term relationship. Because of his willingness to take the long-term view, not only has my friend announced that she will employ him for future tire needs, but her endorsement will likely send many of her friends there as well.

ADAPTING TO THE SITUATION AT HAND

Building credibility often means adapting to new situations and people. Let's say you have a boss who values constant and frequent communication as hallmarks of credibility. So you earn her trust by preparing weekly reports and coming to every meeting highly organized and with a preset agenda. As she likes to be actively involved in the decision-making process, you bring options to her and collaborate on decisions. The process works well.

Then you change organizations.

Your new boss defines credibility differently. He believes in giving you an end result to shoot for and letting you determine how you're going to get there. He's interested in hearing from you if you've hit a roadblock, not in sharing status updates or involving him in all the details. As it turns out, the behaviors you've honed around frequent communication may undermine your credibility in your new role. This ability to observe and reorient oneself is often referred to as situational awareness.

I remember working with a talented account executive who struggled with not being able to adapt. She joined our sales team after running her own company for many years, and quickly landed some very creative and lucrative deals. She had a lot of experience with clients and a great track record of credibility with them.

When it came to my attention that we needed to fill a sales leadership position, her name arose as a possible candidate. As we started the interview process, it became apparent that her selling skills were flawless. She seemed to be the ideal candidate. However, on closer examination, we learned more from her co-workers and boss. While it was true that she outproduced almost every salesperson in the region, the coordinators who worked with her didn't give her such high accolades. They complained about her condescending comments and expressed frustration over how she often put them in urgency mode, only to find out later that it was mostly a ruse to get them to adhere to her timetable.

As we talked with others, a pattern emerged: She was a great salesperson, but she didn't get along very well with the people she needed to work with every day. Her boss decided to hold off on the promotion. When I shared the news with her, she was extremely disappointed. She expressed that she had never been told she had a credibility problem before and had successfully run her own company for years.

While the talented sales professional may have earned credibility as the lone genius, her new circumstance required that she adapt to working with a larger team. Suddenly faced with the prospect of working with others' timelines, skill levels, personalities, and priorities, she wasn't up to the task. She had been too focused on her own agenda rather than the agenda of the whole team. As a result, her credibility suffered, and she missed out on the promotion.

We always pay a price when we lose credibility. While it may be tempting to give up, there's something to be said for staying with it, to be continually behaving our way back to credibility, even when it's been damaged or suffered a blow. It was something I wondered if the mechanic at the tire store my friend Chelsea first visited would come to realize.

• • •

My friend took the second mechanic's advice and ended up saving nearly eight hundred dollars. She also called the original store to not only cancel the appointment but to express her disappointment.

"May I speak with the manager?" she asked after dialing.

"He's not in, but can I help you?" My friend recognized the mechanic who had tried to sell her a thousand dollars' worth of unnecessary tires.

"I've got a concern," she replied. "I came in with a punctured tire yesterday, and you told me I needed to buy a new set of tires."

"Yes, I remember."

"Well, I just want to give you some feedback. I visited another shop, and they not only found that you had incorrectly measured the remaining tread on my tire, but they said I didn't need to replace the whole set. I ended up buying only one tire and had the tread shaved down on it to match

the others. I just wanted you to know it felt like you were trying to take advantage of me. I hope I'm wrong."

My friend later told me she expected to either be hung up on or to hear some choice words back at her.

"Miss," he said into the phone. "I'm sorry. What would you like me to do at this point?"

"Honestly, probably nothing," my friend admitted. "But I appreciate you hearing me out."

Once you've damaged your reputation and credibility with someone, the way back can be difficult, and it certainly won't happen overnight. For my friend, it wasn't too difficult to find another tire vendor. When it comes to relationships, however, people are not so easily replaced. If you've damaged or lost credibility with someone, or if you need to build additional character and competence, begin the process of behaving your way back to credibility today.

BEHAVE YOUR WAY TO CREDIBILITY

So how do you behave your way to credibility?

1. Pick a role or situation in which you would like to increase your credibility.

2. Pick two or three people whose trust you must earn to be credible.

3. Review the suggested qualities that follow, then add other qualities that might be important to those with whom you are trying to increase credibility.

4. Rate yourself on each quality based on how you believe those you've identified would rate you.

Character	LESS									MORE
Models honesty and integrity	1	2	3	4	5	6	7	8	9	10
Is open and humble	1	2	3	4	5	6	7	8	9	10
Considers everyone's interests	1	2	3	4	5	6	7	8	9	10
Shows loyalty	1	2	3	4	5	6	7	8	9	10
Is respectful of others	1	2	3	4	5	6	7	8	9	10
_____	1	2	3	4	5	6	7	8	9	10
_____	1	2	3	4	5	6	7	8	9	10

Competence

Consistently delivers results	1	2	3	4	5	6	7	8	9	10
Is continually improving skills	1	2	3	4	5	6	7	8	9	10
Makes and keeps commitments	1	2	3	4	5	6	7	8	9	10
Expresses ideas with confidence	1	2	3	4	5	6	7	8	9	10
Clarifies expectations	1	2	3	4	5	6	7	8	9	10
_____	1	2	3	4	5	6	7	8	9	10
_____	1	2	3	4	5	6	7	8	9	10

Ask for feedback from those you've identified on how you might increase your credibility with them in any category scoring lower than nine.

PLAY YOUR ROLES WELL

HAVE YOU EVER FOUND THAT SUCCESS IN ONE AREA OF YOUR LIFE COMES AT THE EXPENSE OF ANOTHER AREA?

If so, you may want to consider

PRACTICE 4: PLAY YOUR ROLES WELL.

When you don't play your roles well, your room may feel like Sartre's hell because:

- You constantly feel out of balance and guilty.
- You may neglect an important role for so long that you cause severe relationship damage.
- Life is ultimately unrewarding.

Years ago a good friend of mine, Rachel, went through a divorce. Her ex-husband left her with a mountain of debt that was mostly owed to people she knew in her community. This single mother of two teenage girls had an immediate need to become the family's sole provider. Her father recommended that she consider declaring bankruptcy, but she felt strongly about honoring the commitments that had been made to people she respected. To make ends meet, she took on significantly more hours at her job and gave up whatever free time she had enjoyed before. She was out the door every morning by seven, having made sure her daughters were off to school, and rarely returned home before seven in the evening. After a quick dinner and check-in with her children, she would continue to work late into the night. Her daughters also worked minimum-wage jobs at a local fast-food restaurant. After a couple of years at this pace, along with being exhausted, she was growing distraught about missing important events in her daughters' lives.

One Sunday night while preparing for another marathon workweek, Rachel realized something had to give. She announced to her daughters that she would cut back on a few work projects, recalibrate the rate at which she felt obligated to pay back debts, and commit to being home for dinner by five-thirty each night. One of her daughters replied, "It doesn't matter when you come home, Mom. It seems like even when you're here, you're not really here."

• • •

Like my friend, I can't think of anyone who isn't challenged by trying to balance all the critical roles they play in life; but I know many people who make a deliberate choice to identify their most important roles and pay attention to the contributions they want to make in each of them. As a result, they are rewarded with a greater sense of balance, purpose and, most important, they build richer relationships.

When I say "play" your roles, I don't mean you perform them or fake it, using a written script. Playing a role well means expressing your most authentic and deepest value system through what you do and say. Even when actors are given a fictional part to play, it's only when they bring an authentic part of themselves to the role that they can touch a truth within the human condition. This sentiment was echoed when I had the chance to see one of my favorite plays recently, noting that a critic had given the actress a five-star review. It read, "She authentically embodied the most important qualities of her character."

Even though the majority of us aren't professional thespians, the metaphor of the actor and the stage can still be useful when we evaluate how to play our roles well. William Shakespeare famously wrote, "All the world's a stage, / And all the men and women merely players; / They have their exits and their entrances, / And one man in his time plays many parts . . ."

Reflect on the many roles you play in your life: leader, neighbor, team member, child, parent, friend, coach, sibling, and so on. Imagine if we actually had the opportunity to read a review of our performance in the important roles we play. How many stars would we get? Consider the four people below and how they rate in their various roles.

SALES LEADER ★★

Maria throws herself into the role of leader with enthusiasm. She's driven to win, and it shows in her dissatisfaction with the status quo. But in her hard-charging approach to achieve results, she often misses the subtle clues from team members who need her to slow down and invest in them.

FRIEND ★

Allison commits to bring an appetizer to a friend's dinner party. Everyone but Allison arrives on time. Because this is a pattern with Allison, her friend has already prepared a backup appetizer. While Allison is kind and likable, she has a reputation of being unreliable.

BUSINESS PARTNER ★★★★★

Because of immediate deadlines, it would have been easy for Sarah to shut down her business partner who wanted to develop an app in addition to their core product. But instead, Sarah sat down and took time to hear her out. To her surprise, the partner had a connection to a creative, inexpensive team outside of the country who ended up helping them solve a core-product issue while developing the app. Sarah excelled in her role, putting aside her own biases to consider another point of view.

PARENT ★★

William is the father to three young boys, who treasure their time with him. Driven to compete with the success of a co-worker, William accepts a promotion he doesn't really want and that requires longer hours and significant travel. His choice hits home when William is alone in a hotel room, unable to reach his son on his birthday.

While critical reviews of our roles on a regular basis would be helpful, too often it's only at life's most meaningful milestones (birthdays, funerals, graduations, and so on) that we sit back and take stock. Bronnie Ware experienced this reflection in a unique way as an Australian hospice nurse. She spent several years caring for patients during the last weeks of their lives. She had numerous conversations with them as they took a final look at the various roles they had played. Ware detailed these experiences in her book *The Top Five Regrets of the Dying*, noticing that people in the last stages of life expressed similar patterns of regret. She lists the top five deathbed regrets as:

1. I wish I'd had the courage to live a life true to myself, not the life others expected of me.

2. I wish I hadn't worked so hard.

3. I wish I'd had the courage to express my feelings.

4. I wish I had stayed in touch with my friends.

5. I wish that I had let myself be happier.

While waiting for an interview with someone like Bronnie is one way to take stock of our roles, the benefit of doing it much sooner allows us to actually shape the outcome. To get better at playing your roles well, you need to first identify them, then determine the real contribution you want to make in each one.

IDENTIFY YOUR ROLES

When you consider the roles you currently play at work and home, pay attention to how many you take on. If you've ever watched a one-woman or one-man show, it's a treat to see a single, talented actor seamlessly perform the various parts. But what the actor can't do, no matter how gifted, is play all of them well at the same time. Unfortunately, we wildly overestimate our ability to effectively focus on several things at once. The only thing that comes from working on too many roles at the same time is mediocrity. For instance, I can work on a critical email in my role as project leader while I pretend to listen to an employee on the phone as he or she pours out his or her heart to me, but who am I kidding? When I try to multitask, neither role gets my full attention or authenticity. And the others involved always sense it.

Some of my most important roles are father, son, grandfather, leader, spouse, community volunteer, and business coach. Some examples of other professional roles might include team leader, writer, accountant, assistant, teacher, software engineer, marketing manager, attorney, counselor, and so on. Personal roles might be sister, soccer coach, spouse or life partner, hospice volunteer, artist, swimmer, friend, or world traveler. You get to choose which roles need the most attention at any given time. Remember, it's not about spending equal time in each role (most people will spend more hours at work each week than they will on a hobby or an important relationship), but it is about regularly keeping your most important roles top of mind and ensuring you have an overall balance in the long run. Realize that some roles stay with you for a lifetime (parent, partner, friend), and others may change over time (jobs, community volunteer positions, and so on). Quite often our long-term roles turn out to be where we experience the most character and relationship growth.

Choosing meaningful roles isn't something someone does for you; it's something you do based on your value system. Sometimes, especially around career choices, we end up in roles someone else has prioritized for us.

A good friend of mine grew up watching her dad, Paul, run a successful family-owned bakery. The bakery business is a time-intensive and physically demanding job. Paul woke up every morning at four, six days a week, to drive to work and heft twenty-five-pound bags of flour around to measure the ingredients and knead the dough before the bakery opened at seven. After the morning rush, he would clean the ovens and kitchen and prepare for lunchtime customers. Throughout the day, he would make trips back and forth between the hot ovens and the freezers, preparing ingredients and freezing dough, only to completely clean the kitchen from top to bottom one more time (including all the various bowls, mixers, and utensils), just to start the process over again the next morning. Most of the work was done in isolation—with only one or two employees assisting him or helping customers at the front counter. As a married man with two small children, Paul felt an immediate need to provide for his family and be there to watch over his aging father who had worked hard at keeping the business alive. While it was important to contribute to his role as husband and son, Paul wasn't happy working in the bakery.

Not only was the work grueling and tedious, but the long hours meant he was spending little time with his family (and when he was, he was too exhausted to do much). Paul was also an extrovert who loved being around people. The isolation of the bakery job didn't allow him to express his innate social gifts. As the years dragged on, Paul became more tired and depressed. Being a good husband, father, and son were part of the values that meant the most to him, but he realized he'd lost the proper balance. The bakery had become all-consuming, leaving little time and energy for anything else. He made a radical change in midlife: He sold the bakery and took a job as a paper salesman. On the surface, this switch seemed like an odd career choice, but Paul was suddenly much happier than he'd been in years. He worked regular hours, left the physically demanding aspects of his previous job behind, and started using his friendly, extroverted people skills to create a successful new professional path. Most important, he was more fulfilled at work, and therefore more available for his spouse and family. When the roles we play slip out of congruence with who we are, then it's worth making a change. Remember the number-one regret from those at the end of their lives: *I wish I'd had the courage to live a life true to myself, not the life others expected of me.*

On one end of the continuum is focusing on too many roles at once. On the other end is becoming too myopic—excelling in one role at the expense of others. For instance, a colleague of mine, Ruben, shared his own struggle with this practice as a young executive. Having accepted a new role, the nearly crushing weight of the sudden responsibilities had overtaken his life. He spent his days, as he put it, "Putting out fires and slaying dragons." Working late one day, an appointment reminder interrupted Ruben. He looked at his calendar and saw that he was scheduled to meet his wife and children for a family picture. He knew his wife had signed up for a package that allowed for several group sittings, so he decided to cancel this one. He called his wife, despite the fact it was short notice, and explained that he had too much to do at the office and that she needed to reschedule the appointment. She replied that she understood and would take care of it. With his calendar now cleared, Ruben went back to work, grateful for the time he had managed to reclaim.

A couple of months later, on Christmas Day, he sat with his family and opened gifts. Ruben was handed a present with his name on it, and upon unwrapping it, found a beautifully framed family portrait. But there was something missing from the picture—Ruben! His wife, with only good intentions, had decided to keep the appointment after all. As he stared at the picture, noting his absence, he realized his focus on his work role was starting to come at the expense of his roles as husband and father. The picture, minus him, was a not-so-gentle reminder that his priorities were off. "I had forgotten what mattered most," he shared with me in retrospect. "Work would wait. Being part of my family's life would not. I never wanted to be missing from a family picture again."

Ruben shared that he'd also failed to realize the impact of canceling the appointment just thirty minutes before the scheduled sitting. With three daughters under six, his wife had spent the preceding hours getting the girls bathed, doing their hair, dressing them in newly purchased clothes, then trying to keep them in their pristine state. My friend had failed to take a step back, to consider the larger picture, and to account for how a singular focus on one role was about to impact several others. The family picture still hangs in his office as a reminder.

It might be tempting to believe that work is always cast as the bad guy when it comes to prioritizing our roles. I firmly believe and have seen that you can be contributing, engaged, and highly productive in your career, as well as exceptional in your personal roles (five-star reviews in both). It's a matter of prioritization, and it may mean giving up a hobby, the night out with some colleagues, and so forth. In the end, you have to sacrifice somewhere, but being mindful of balance is key.

Once you've identified your most meaningful roles, you're able to determine how and when you want to show up in those roles. When it comes to prioritization and focus, consider how an air-traffic controller lands an airplane. At any given moment, there may be dozens of aircraft in motion—taxiing, taking off, or landing. Each one is very important and the controller must be aware of all the planes on the radar, yet it would be a mistake (and impossible) to focus on all of them equally. At the critical moment of landing, only one plane warrants the controller's full talents, attention, and expertise. To serve all the planes and their passengers with excellence, the controller must focus on and land just one airplane at a time. So it is with our most important roles: We should never lose sight of them on our radar, but we should also be prepared to give our full attention to the one that needs it most at any particular time.

DETERMINE YOUR CONTRIBUTION IN EACH ROLE

Because we have any number of tasks to perform each day, it might be easier to start thinking of roles in terms of to-do lists. But that is a mistake. Roles go much deeper. Our roles are never just about what we do but are ways through which we express our values and who we are at our core. Roles require much more than to-dos. They require "to-bes" as well. A to-do is a task that usually has a beginning and an end. A to-be is an ongoing value or a character quality we're striving to become or at which to get better. Consider our imaginary critic writing a review as we go about performing our roles. How would that critic describe who we are—our character qualities? Are we self-serving or selfless? ambitious or amiable? egotistical or egalitarian (or two other opposing words that start with the same letter)? If an outside observer can't connect our actions to our values, we're doing something wrong. In "Practice 7: Think We, Not Me," I share the power of taking time to consider intent, both ours and others'. We can do something similar when we prepare to work within our various roles by drafting what is called a *contribution statement*. Doing so helps us stay grounded in our values and works to ensure that we are doing the things that matter most: building and nurturing our most important and meaningful relationships.

A contribution statement about how we want to be in each role lays the foundation for what we call a "personal mission statement." It expresses our purpose and values, and becomes the standard by which we measure everything else in our lives. Consider some of the following role contribution statements and how they relate to each person's fundamental values.

Parent: I will create a place of unconditional love, safety, and
    empowerment so my children can express their potential and
    become responsible adults.

Engineer: I will find new ways to provide safe drinking water
    for everyone in my community and help make policies that

dramatically improve how we recycle so that our planet will thrive.

Manager: I will be the leader who develops our company's next generation of leaders.

Architect: I will create an artistic legacy in my city.

Friend: I will listen patiently without judgment and look for ways to support, forgive, and help.

Musician: I will ensure that the arts remain central to the lives of people in our community.

Teacher: I will strive to identify and unleash the passion for reading and learning in my students.

Project Manager: I will be the one people come to when they want it done right.

Adult Child: I will be patient, kind, and considerate when caring for my aging parents and dedicate time to visit them each week.

Business Coach: I will view everyone I coach as capable, resourceful, and whole—not someone I need to fix—so that they begin to experience their own potential.

Self: I will consistently set and keep commitments to my physical, emotional, mental, and spiritual well-being.

Notice that I added self as a role. As we continue to explore Sartre's notion as to how we approach our relationships being the key to hell or happiness, we should be mindful of ourselves as well. The reason airline safety procedures direct you to put on your oxygen mask first in an emergency is not because you're more important than the people around you, but that you can't help anyone else if you don't take care of yourself first. Without taking care of yourself, you won't be able to show up for anyone else. Your *wholeness* will not be there. Take time to deepen your knowledge of yourself—your dreams, desired contributions, character qualities. Also keep in mind the health of your body, mind, social/emotional condition, and spiritual life.

No one can tell you how to live your roles or which contributions you should make. They will be unique to you. After a late-night flight to Chicago for an early morning client meeting, I was a feeling a little foggy when the meeting began. We met in an ornate boardroom, complete with a large mahogany table and red leather chairs. There was an air of formality about the room. As our clients filed in and we introduced ourselves, I noticed one gentleman—a gray-haired executive in his early fifties—carrying a bright orange notebook. Now, I don't mean to suggest this notebook had a subtle hue that represented the cusp of some new fashion sensibility, but rather the kind of bold, bright, triumphant orange perfectly suited to a safety vest. Given the old-world stylings of the room and buttoned-down nature of the meeting, the notebook might as well have been a flashing neon sign.

As we took our places around the table, my eyes kept drifting to the notebook's cover; it had to signify something, or was I reading too much into it because of being a little jet-lagged? I mean, who was I to judge if the man liked radiant orange? I then watched as this distinguished gentleman removed his cellphone and placed it dutifully next to the notebook—a phone wrapped in an equally brilliant orange protector.

After the meeting concluded, I approached the man and thanked him for hosting us. And because I couldn't help myself, I motioned toward his notebook and phone. "That's kind of a unique color," I prompted. The man smiled in return.

"Yes, it is."

"Does it have some meaning, if you don't mind my asking?"

The man nodded. "As a matter of fact, it does. It reminds me that no matter what I'm doing at the office, no matter how rough things get at work, I have another role that's even more important."

The answer from this seasoned executive surprised me. He smiled at my reaction, something he was probably practiced at, then continued: "Ever since my daughter was a child, she's loved this color. I can't really explain it, but she's attracted to anything with this color orange in it. She loves it so much that my wife and I allowed her to pick one section of her bedroom wall and paint it construction-sign orange. We did it over a weekend together, and it's one of my favorite memories. So I found a notebook and cellphone cover in the same orange and now carry them everywhere I go. And no matter how overwhelmed I may become with numerous problems at work, I always see these and they remind me of my family. It's just a simple thing, right? But it helps me to never lose sight of what matters most in my life."

I was impressed. This executive had found a unique way of reminding himself of his important role as father. And I'm assuming from this simple yet meaningful symbol, he also focuses on balancing all of his important roles, both personal and professional, to ensure he plays them well. Although we were brought in to help the organization solve a problem of theirs, I couldn't help but think I may have gotten the better half of the deal. It reminded me of my friend Rachel and her struggle to balance the roles she was playing in her life.

● ● ●

One Sunday night while preparing for another marathon work week, Rachel realized something had to give. She announced to her daughters that she would cut back on a few work projects, recalibrate the rate at which she felt obligated to pay back debts, and commit to being home for dinner by five-thirty each night. One of her daughters replied, "It doesn't matter when you come home, Mom. It seems like even when you're here, you're not really here."

The reality of her daughter's comment invited Rachel to step back and examine the other important roles she needed to play. The role of mother had taken a hit. As a result, she took time to evaluate her approach. Like the analogy of the air-traffic controller, Rachel realized she was in a critical moment for prioritizing one role (that of being a mother) while not losing sight of the rest. After some soul searching, she had a brilliant idea. She convinced the girls to quit their fast-food jobs and work for her part-time in an administrative capacity. Since her employer regularly hired hosts and registrants to work the various events she led, she asked if her girls could take those responsibilities on. Over time, many of the long days apart be-

came time working together, and the family bonded and grew in remarkable ways. Because my friend had focused on her role as a provider when it was necessary, she managed to weather a serious financial storm. Additionally, she took the time to step back and assess the other roles in her life. When the moment was right, she made a meaningful change and found balance through strengthening her relationship with her daughters.

PLAY YOUR ROLES WELL

1. Identify five to seven of your important roles. Be sure to include a mix of professional and personal.

2. For each role, identify someone you significantly influence when you are in that role (e.g., if it's the role of parent, you'd choose a child; if it's the role of leader, you would choose a member of the team).

3. Write a short paragraph from the perspective of the person influenced by you. What would that person say if he or she gave you a five-star rating? In other words, what contribution do you want to make in that role?

4. Identify one thing you will do this week to start making your ideal a reality.

ROLE	IMPORTANT PEOPLE INFLUENCED	CONTRIBUTION STATEMENT
1. Mother	Daughter	Live and behave in a way that demonstrates to my daughter she is a priority.
2. Leader	Team Member	I will communicate to my team member through my words and actions that I believe in his potential.
3.		
4.		
5.		
6.		
7.		

SEE THE TREE, NOT JUST THE SEEDLING

WITH PEOPLE, DO YOU OFTEN CONCLUDE THAT "WHAT YOU SEE IS WHAT YOU GET"?

If so, you may want to consider

PRACTICE 5: SEE THE TREE, NOT JUST THE SEEDLING.

When you see just the seedling and not the tree, your room may feel like Sartre's hell because:

- Your limiting beliefs become reality.
- Growth is stunted in yourself and others.
- You're continually looking elsewhere for talent that may be right in front of you.

Rhonda sent me three texts in less than thirty minutes, which was definitely not the norm. I had been stuck in an important meeting, so I couldn't break away, despite her somewhat cryptic message: "Making a personnel change on my team. Call me."

After wrapping things up, I found I had some time before my next commitment, so I headed down to her office. I suspected a face-to-face conversation might be better than a call. I found Rhonda at her desk reviewing papers, a yellow highlighter in one hand and a red pen in the other. She looked up at me over her reading glasses and raised an eyebrow. "So you are in the office today," she teased. Rhonda assumed everyone had an innate capacity to multitask as well as she could, and had she ever announced that she'd come from a long line of circus jugglers, I wouldn't have been surprised.

"Sorry I couldn't get back to you," I said, "but I do have a few minutes now if that works."

"Shouldn't take too long," she said.

I shut the door behind me and took a seat. "So personnel changes?" I prompted.

"Pretty much. I need to let Ava go, and I know I can't just do that without jumping through all the HR hoops." I pushed the image of circus performers out of my mind. "Whatever we have to do to check the box and let her go," she continued. "I know there's a protocol we have to follow for this sort of thing, so what's the quickest way we can get it done?"

"Okay, I hear you," I replied, "but how about we slow things down a little. Why don't you tell me what's going on?"

Rhonda sighed, putting her pen down. "You know the old saying, 'A chain is only as strong as its weakest link?'"

"I'm familiar with it."

"It's as simple as that: Ava is the weak link on our team. She's not pulling her weight, Todd, and I don't know if she's incapable or lazy or maybe both. But I do know she just doesn't have what it takes to succeed, and while it may sound unfair, I've heard from others that she's basically worthless. She just doesn't have the potential for this job."

• • •

Rhonda's situation certainly wasn't unique. I've had similar discussions with other managers over the years who have basically given up on a team member. Sometimes a person is truly misaligned for a role and a change needs to be made. But while making a change is often the go-to thinking, a true misalignment is not always the case. It's human nature to get frustrated with someone's behavior and want to write the person off, especially if he or she isn't doing the job the way you think it should be done. Such was the case for Joseph Degenhart, a Greek grammar teacher who had become furious at the behavior of one of his students—an unruly boy who had a reputation for telling jokes and cutting class. Degenhart went so far as to make the case that the child be expelled from school. He wrote a devastating note: "Nothing will ever become of you. Your mere presence here undermines the class's respect for me."

The student, as it turned out, was Albert Einstein.

But the story continues. Because of such poor references, Einstein barely squeaked into college. It was there, however, that he met a more senior student who saw great potential in him. The student's name was Michelangelo Besso, and he also studied physics. It was unusual for an upperclassman like Besso to take an interest in such a junior classmate, but their friendship became the closest of Einstein's life. Besso not only helped the struggling Einstein get a job, but they had frequent engaging discussions about science. Einstein found in Besso a true listener, a sounding board for his ideas about the universe. It was during these talks with Besso that Einstein made his great leap of discovery—the astounding idea that there must be almost unlimited energy packed within every atom of matter. That led to the discovery of atomic power and reframed how we came to think about the universe. Later Besso would remark that "Einstein the eagle took Besso the sparrow under his wing, and the sparrow flew a little higher."[6] Hardly anyone remembers Besso now, but without Besso's belief in

Einstein, "the eagle," the world may have missed out on one of the greatest thinkers in human history.

When we look at a person's potential—whether it's a co-worker, direct report, friend, partner, or child—it requires us to see past the "seed" and envision the mighty tree it can become. Seeing potential in others is a paradigm that recognizes growth as an organic principle. It doesn't happen overnight; it's a function of growth over time. After years of watching and helping others grow in their careers and relationships, I have come to believe that people are fundamentally resourceful, capable, and whole—a view that stands in stark contrast with the notion that people are broken, incapable, or needing to be fixed.

I recall an incident earlier in my career where a boss saw me not only for who I was, but also for what I was capable of. I had been employed as a recruitment manager for what was then called Covey Leadership Center. It was my thirty-fifth day of employment—and while I can't recall much of what happened on Day Thirty-Four or Thirty-Six, I do remember Day Thirty-Five with great clarity. After an early morning company meeting, my boss Pam introduced me to one of the members of the senior-leadership team. As we shook hands, she announced, "Let me tell you what Todd has accomplished during his first thirty-five days with us."

I panicked and couldn't imagine what she was about to say: I couldn't think of *one thing* I'd done during the past thirty-five days that warranted attention from a member of the senior-leadership team. Sick to my stomach, I listened as Pam continued: "Todd filled the sales position in Chicago that has been vacant for the past six months, he's drafted a relocation policy we've needed for quite some time, he's created a recruitment strategy for the coming year . . ." And the list went on.

Now, I don't share this story to boast about my successes. I share it because I remember that moment like it was yesterday. While I realized that I had accomplished the things Pam was describing, I was in shock that she took such an active interest in what I was doing. I remember thinking at the time, *This woman believes I can do anything!* That belief resonated in me for years to come, and I made it a priority to exceed her expectations with anything and everything she asked. Pam truly believed in me—more than I believed in myself—and I wasn't about to prove her wrong.

Chances are you've been on the receiving end of someone who recognized and believed in your potential—seeing the tree, not just the seedling. It may have come from a parent, a sibling, a teacher, or even a boss. Dr. Covey summed up his own experience with the man who started him down the path that ultimately led to his life's work: "His ability to see more in me than I saw in myself—his willingness to entrust me with responsibility that would stretch me to my potential—unlocked something in me." This powerful experience led to Dr. Stephen R. Covey's often-repeated maxim: "Leadership is communicating to people their worth and potential so clearly that they come to see it themselves."

You may recall the story of my daughter Sydney in the first practice, and my struggles to help her complete a marathon. I have a distinct memory of the two of us going to the video store when she was a child. (If you don't know what a video store is, imagine Netflix as a retail shop where movies are downloaded onto large spools of magnetic tape for your convenience.) Sydney was eight years old at the time, and given her hearing loss, her mother and I were the only two people who could readily understand her when she spoke. Nevertheless, my precocious little girl was determined that *she* was going to be the one to ask the video-store clerk to find the Disney movie she had in mind. I immediately became anxious; I had no idea how this stranger would react to her inability to speak clearly, or how that might, in turn, affect my daughter. As her father, I wanted to protect her from experiencing the pain she was certain to encounter—to shield her self-esteem from any of the bruises that might result. But this little girl would not be swayed, and she approached the counter determined. She confidently announced the movie she wanted. Her speech was unclear as she pressed too many words together, lacking the normal diction one learns while growing up hearing others speak.

The confused video clerk turned his head, unable to understand her. "I'm sorry, what did you say?"

I wanted to leap to her defense. It would have been easy enough to do, and would save her any further pain or embarrassment. But Sydney pressed on, repeating her words a second time. The clerk looked at me, inviting me to interpret what my daughter was asking for. But before I could jump in, my daughter grabbed hold of the counter and tried again.

"I'm so sorry, I still don't understand," the clerk replied. I couldn't imagine what this felt like for this precious eight-year-old. I practically willed her to give up and turn around—I knew all it would take was one imploring look, and I could jump in and solve the situation. But she didn't. She took a breath, and again let the words tumble from her mouth the best she could. This attempt at communication happened over and over. The clerk, to his credit, continued to try his best to understand. But each time he came up short, unable to piece together the words my daughter was attempting to say. I watched, unsure of what to do. I worried that each attempt was only going to make the final defeat more painful. My daughter, undeterred, made the seventh attempt. I wondered how long this back-and-forth could continue. But something registered in the clerk's expression—he managed to catch hold of a word from within the sounds my daughter was making.

"Mermaid . . . ? *The Little Mermaid*? Is that what you'd like?" he asked.

My daughter nodded excitedly, looking triumphant as the clerk retrieved the tape. In that moment, I realized the limiting view that had crept into my perception of Sydney. She wasn't broken, incapable, or needing to be fixed. Certainly, she had her challenges, but I had forgotten that this amazing child had lived with her disability since she was a baby. She had learned to overcome it time and time again. This was a girl who possessed the strength and potential to achieve whatever she wanted in life! My paradigm changed when I came to see my daughter as someone with much more potential than I had previously allowed. Had I stepped in to help her, even with my good intentions, it would have undermined everything she was working for. In trying to help, I might have decreased her potential, perhaps slowing her growth from a seedling into a magnificent tree. There is power in failure. Standing alone at the video-store counter, Sydney had the opportunity to try and fail without someone taking over. When I held back, it sent a different message—a message that I believed in her. And even though I was paralyzed with fear, it had been a serendipitous moment because it allowed me to recognize what she was capable of.

Seeing potential in others isn't just about *hoping* people will succeed. It's believing they have unlimited talents, abilities, and opportunities for growth. It's also understanding that the road to success is paved with failures—that growing is an ongoing process that may take a lifetime. When we take the long-term view, we see that failure can be a moment of instruction and reflection and can serve to increase the likelihood of success. Failure is an important and necessary function of growth and is precisely the reason I didn't call this practice *See the Tree, Not Just the Seedling Only When People Make No Mistakes and Do Everything Right the First Time.*

Allowing ourselves to see potential in others is also not about flattery—it's not about being the rah-rah person who goes around giving everyone high fives and telling them they're great. On the opposite end of the spectrum, seeing potential isn't about continually correcting performance or focusing on all the risks and mistakes that stand in the way of someone's potential. A colleague of mine once described feeling that his leader was running alongside of him, constantly telling him how to ride a bike: *Don't forget to wear a helmet, remember to look both ways, watch out for cars—you're about to crash!* It may feel like we're being helpful, focusing on the negative to keep others from taking a spill, but we're not. To see the potential in others requires us to believe that the seed, with the right kind of nourishment, will become the mighty oak.

Consider the following questions regarding how you think about others:

- Do you tend only to notice the weaknesses in others, or try to constantly encourage them to engage their strengths?
- Do you make it a point to catch people doing good things, or tend to wait to expose them when they fail?

- Do you encourage people to rise to new challenges, or discourage them from taking a risk?
- Do you jump in to correct at the first sign of failure, or give people time and opportunities to show what they can do?

AT THE HEART OF THESE QUESTIONS IS THE UNDERSTANDING THAT WE CAN ALL HAVE AN INFLUENCE ON EACH OTHER. I'M REMINDED OF A QUOTE ONCE SHARED WITH ME:

"IN EVERYONE'S LIFE, AT SOME TIME, OUR INNER FIRE GOES OUT.

"IT IS THEN BURST INTO FLAME BY AN ENCOUNTER WITH ANOTHER HUMAN BEING."

—ALBERT SCHWEITZER

Let's face it, the fact that you're reading a book like this one (and not, say, *The Narcissist's Guide to Shameless Self-Promotion*) says something about you; that is, you care about the relationships around you. I don't know if your inner fire is burning brightly. What I do know is that there is power in seeing potential in others and, at that moment of contact—when one flame lights another—both end up shining a little brighter. It was this perspective I hoped to share with my colleague Rhonda.

● ● ●

"It's as simple as that: Ava is the weak link on our team. She's not pulling her weight, Todd, and I don't know if she's incapable or lazy or maybe both. But I do know she just doesn't have what it takes to succeed, and while it may sound unfair, I've heard from others on my team that she's basically worthless. She just doesn't have the potential for this job."

I sat back and considered Rhonda's position. Certainly, I needed to be open to the fact that sometimes there are misalignments between people and their roles. But I wasn't convinced a misalignment was the case, at least not yet. "So Rhonda, tell me about yourself," I began.

Rhonda seemed surprised by the question. "Me . . .?"

"I mean, you're one of the most efficient and effective people I know. Have you always been that way?"

"Not always," she admitted. "But my mom . . . Now there was a lady who knew how to get things done. If you grew up in a house like that, you learned a few things—like setting high expectations for everything and everyone."

I nodded. "It seems like that experience has served you well."

"I suppose," she offered guardedly, "but this isn't about me."

"No," I replied. "But I wonder if Ava ever had a similar model to draw from?"

Rhonda stared at me blankly. "I honestly have no idea. And really, I'm not sure it matters."

"Okay, fair enough," I said. "But let me ask you about something you said. You indicated that members of your team referred to her as 'worthless.' I can't imagine they meant she has no value as a human being. Were they talking about her value in her role? I want to press you a little here; is that really true? Isn't there anything she does right?"

Rhonda shrugged. "Well, of course there is. She's pleasant enough with people. And to be fair, she has to work with some really strong personalities."

"I've heard positive things from others about how easy she is to work with," I said.

"Even so, we have numbers to hit," Rhonda added. "She may be pleasant, but I need things to get done."

"My understanding is that she moved the entire Certification Project online, and with no major glitches," I added.

"Sure, eventually," Rhonda said. "The problem isn't really the quality of her work, it's that I have to be on her all the time for her to get it finished."

"So if I understand what you're saying," I continued, "Ava has good people skills and can do high-quality work. It's just that she isn't proactive,

and you're spending too much time managing her. Is that right, or am I missing something?"

"Sounds about right," Rhonda admitted.

"And while Ava has areas in which she needs to improve, and you can't continue to spend all your time following up on her, I don't believe you are saying you're unwilling to help people grow."

"No, that's not what I'm saying at all."

"I didn't think so. I wonder if you would be open to something. Would it would be possible to take the next thirty days and put the past aside?" I offered. "I realize it sounds like we're slowing down, but just hear me out. Ava is good with people and has some strong skills, but she needs coaching around being proactive. Let's see what she may or may not be able to do. Worst case is that we've at least given it one last shot."

"Coaching?" Rhonda pushed, raising an eyebrow.

"I'm suggesting we have a choice: We can either see Ava as being fundamentally flawed in this role, or see her as a person with untapped potential."

"So, what are you suggesting?"

"That you have a conversation with her. Start by saying you can see Ava as being wildly successful in her role, but that something is standing in the way. Let her know that you value how easy she is to work with, and that you appreciate her capabilities on things like the Certification Project, but also let her know that you need her to be a lot more proactive. I suspect that you may even need to share with her what you mean by proactive. Give her some specific examples tied to her role. Because being proactive isn't a natural strength of hers, she'll benefit from you pointing out exactly what you mean."

Rhonda thought it over and nodded. "I suppose I can do that."

Four weeks later, Rhonda returned to my office. I knew she had been working with Ava and I was anxious to hear the results.

"So how is it going?" I asked.

"To be honest, it was a little awkward at first," Rhonda admitted. "I suppose it says something about me needing to do a better job coaching each member of my team. But in the end, I took your advice. I told Ava I saw potential in her and that there was something standing in the way. I *also did as you suggested and shared a time when I was given some tough feedback. And although it stung a little, I was ultimately able to make some changes that served me well throughout my career."*

"And how did she take it?"

"Well, I realized about halfway through the conversation that I was doing all the talking and that she had shut down. So I stopped and asked what was important to her in her role and career. It ended up being a great discussion, and she really opened up. Anyway, we talked about how being proactive would help her achieve what she wanted while also addressing my concerns. And while I haven't yet made up my mind, I've been impressed with how she's starting to do certain things differently. Not perfectly, but she's made some pretty drastic improvements."

"So where is your thinking now around letting her go?"

"Again, she's not where she needs to be, but she is off to a great start. I'm hopeful that things will continue to get better and better."

SEE THE TREE, NOT JUST THE SEEDLING

When you believe in the potential of others, you help them see more clearly what they are capable of, engage their strengths and talents that may be lying dormant, and ultimately allow them to become the people they want to be.

Identify two or three people with whom you struggle to see their full potential. Similar to the example below, list the current beliefs or paradigms you have about each person's capabilities, talents, skills, and style. Then answer the questions in the last two columns.

RELATIONSHIP	LIMITING BELIEFS OR PARADIGMS	CHALLENGE YOUR CURRENT THINKING: WHAT DO THEY DO WELL? WHAT MIGHT THEY NEED TO REACH THEIR POTENTIAL (A NEW SITUATION, COACHING, ETC.)? WHAT WOULD THEIR GREATEST FAN SAY ABOUT THEM?	WHAT CAN I DO TO SUPPORT THIS PERSON?
Tyler	Tyler is a follower, not a leader. He lacks the confidence he needs for people to want to follow him.	-Tyler follows through on every assignment. He is punctual. He doesn't gossip about others. -Tyler needs small leadership experiences that give him confidence. He needs more positive feedback on what he is doing well now. -Tyler can do anything if you give him a chance to contribute. He has a good heart and great integrity. He's someone you can count on.	1. Write Tyler a note expressing appreciation for what I've seen him do well. 2. Consider giving Tyler a small project to lead next quarter.

AVOID THE PINBALL SYNDROME

DO YOU EVER REACH THE END OF THE DAY AND FEEL AS THOUGH NOTHING OF REAL VALUE HAS BEEN ACCOMPLISHED?

If so, you may want to consider

PRACTICE 6: AVOID THE PINBALL SYNDROME.

When you don't avoid the pinball syndrome, your room may feel like Sartre's hell because:

- You don't realize where you've ended up until it's too late.
- You're so busy fighting fires, you spend no time preventing them.
- You never beat the pinball game and often end up feeling like the ball.

Melissa cared about being a positive influence in the world. She had worked diligently over a career spanning nearly two decades, and now led a critical channel for the organization and had several direct reports. So I was a bit surprised when Garret, a longtime member of her team, approached me.

"You know I think Melissa is a good person," he confided, something obviously weighing heavily on him. "I really do appreciate her on many levels. But I have some concerns about how we work together. And to be honest, for the first time in ten years, I'm starting to think about moving to a different department." He shared more with me and gave me permission to talk to Melissa after she'd canceled several appointments to meet with him. And that was the kind of thing he'd been experiencing. He went on to inform me that he wasn't the only person feeling this way. It confirmed some patterns I had also noticed. I thanked Garret for his candor and decided I'd approach the subject with Melissa at a scheduled meeting we had the following day.

We met in my office, and after a couple of minutes exchanging pleasantries, I asked Melissa if she was okay if we used the time to discuss an issue not included on our agenda. "Of course," she replied. If she was sensing something was amiss on her team, she wasn't showing it. "There's plenty on my to-do list, but I can always spare a few minutes for you." I smiled at that comment—I'd had plenty of people say something similar over the years, but with Melissa, it was always sincere. It was part of her charm, which made the topic of our discussion even more perplexing.

"Thanks," I continued. "I've been hesitant to share this feedback because I wanted to make sure I really understood what I wanted to convey. I hope you know that my only intent in sharing this with you is to help you be successful."

"Okay," Melissa said, leaning forward in her chair. "You've now got me a little nervous. But go on."

"Garret came to me yesterday and shared some concerns he and other members of the team are having. He's so frustrated that, after ten years of working here, he's starting to think about switching to a different department."

"Wow! You know that's the last thing I want."

"I do, and I'd like to help if I can. Do you mind if I share some observations?"

"Of course not."

"So Melissa, what I see in you is someone who's passionate about her work and the company, and you have absolutely no ego despite your many accomplishments. And while you consistently hit your department goals, I think you may be losing the hearts and minds of your team along the way."

Melissa frowned. "Garret said all that?"

"Not in so many words, but I think it accurately reflects how he's feeling. And while I don't believe anyone questions your intentions, there is a sense that you choose to focus on tasks over people. I wonder if that is why you end up canceling so many meetings with your team members. One of the reasons Garret came to me was he couldn't get on your calendar."

"I'm really sorry to hear that," Melissa replied as her phone gave off a ping. She glanced down at the message, and I waited while she scanned it before silencing her device. "Sorry about that, but you see how busy things are. In a perfect world, I'd love to have regular one-on-one meetings with everyone on my team, I really would. But that's just not reality. Honestly, I don't have the time."

● ● ●

On a recent drive to work, I couldn't help but notice a driver in the next lane who seemed to be in a tremendous hurry. At each intersection, we both waited for the light to change. But at the first sign of the green light—as if we were competitors at a drag strip—he punched the gas, lurched across the intersection, and raced toward the line of cars in the distance. I, however, accelerated at a pace appropriate for someone whose idea of thrill-seeking is staying up to watch late-night television. When I reached the line of commuters ahead, I pulled next to the anxious driver (whose own quarter-mile sprint hadn't taken him past the upcoming traffic or light) and waited for the light to change again. I glanced at the man through the corner of my eye and saw him pressed forward in his seat, staring at the stoplight as if he could turn it green through an act of sheer willpower. The light changed and the man raced ahead. I caught up to him yet again. This back-and-forth continued for some time as we moved from light to light, one intersection at a time. I wondered if the driver would ever see the futility of his approach.

The experience made me think about how often we chase after metaphorical stoplights in our own lives, stomping on the gas and racing ahead block after block, without even noticing the impact on others around us. What if such a hyperfocus limits us from stepping back and examining the road itself? And just where is that road taking us? It was with such thoughts that I considered a former associate of mine at a previous company. The occasion was his funeral.

On a gray winter afternoon, I pondered the life of the man being laid to rest. He had invested most of his life in a company he founded and had been recognized for many professional accomplishments. Starting a company takes a lot of time; urgencies abound, and a focus on the immediate can make the difference between a company's success or failure. I reflected on a conversation we'd had many years before, when he mentioned that while he intended the urgencies to be temporary, they had regrettably become a way of life. His "season of imbalance," as he liked to call it, had extended to over thirty years.

As I listened to what seemed to be perfunctory remarks about himself and his devotion to his job, I was struck with the notion that in two or three days, life would continue. The to-do lists, the meetings, the client visits, and all the activities that made up his workday would matter-of-factly be picked up by somebody else. The job would go on. I then took note of the man's family: His adult children sat stoically as the mostly generic eulogy was delivered, and his estranged ex-wife sat with her new husband. Behind them, rows of conspicuously empty seats marked the poor turnout. Here was the funeral of a man who had worked hard to rise to an important and respected position—traveling the world, managing teams, and, by some accounts, finding success.

However, looking at his family, it appeared that all his professional accomplishments and all the urgent to-dos seemed to have come at a heavy price.

I contrasted this experience with another funeral I attended earlier in the year. The woman being laid to rest had worked in an administrative-support role at her company. She'd never held a prominent title, managed others, or traveled to some interesting locale on company business. Yet, she seemed to embody the very principles I've sought to write about in this book. Her family had even gone to great lengths to accelerate and reschedule the wedding plans of her son so she could attend that important event before her death. The funeral service was packed with co-workers, friends, family, and those whose lives she had positively affected. Gratitude and love permeated the gathering as story after story illustrated how this unassuming woman had invested in others. And while saying goodbye to her was difficult, everyone who attended the funeral walked away with the impression that this beautiful soul had left behind a life well lived.

Reflecting on the funerals, it occurred to me that the main difference between these two people was how they had prioritized. One had unintentionally allowed urgencies to come at the expense of important relationships. The other one had made relationship building a part of her life's work. It made me wonder: What distracts us from those things we've decided are truly important? Why are we willing to exchange the timeless for the transitory? Giving in to the allure of the urgent over the important is what I call *the pinball syndrome*.

Think back to the last time you played a pinball game. While there are plenty of pinball apps available, I'm thinking specifically about the games that had their heydays in the late seventies and early eighties. These were masterfully crafted machines, representing a blend of the fantastical, mechanical, and electronic. Here's how they work: The pinball player's goal is to use two or more flippers (small movable bars) to launch a metal ball into numerous physical targets, accumulating points, and unlocking various rewards. These visually beautiful games are designed to engage the senses: Lights flash as large scoreboards track progress, while bells ding, bumpers thump, and the ball clacks and rolls across wood and metal tracks. It's a very visceral experience, and it's easy for the sights and sounds to drown out one's senses and demand complete attention. Eventually, gravity will win the day, however, as the ball slips past the frantically swinging flippers and drops out of sight. But fear not, for there's always a new ball ready to ratchet into place. All we have to do is pull the plunger back and send it on its way.

The truth is that with practically every worthwhile job or career, we can all get caught up in the pinball syndrome. Think of a pinball machine as a metaphor for all the urgent things that demand our attention throughout the day. And while we may not feel like we're playing a game, per se, when accomplishing such tasks, we might feel attracted to (or even seduced by) the rapid pace and focus that's required to get them done. Add a small endorphin rush as we check off the next item on our to-do list, and it's easy to see how the urgent can feel gratifying, even addictive at times. The challenge is that some of the urgencies might also be important, but the allure of the game gives everything equal weight. As a result, we can end up spending time and energy on the less important. In the words of author J. K. Rowling's Albus Dumbledore, "Humans have a knack for choosing precisely the things that are worst for them."

Urgent things act on us; they compete for our attention and insist on a response. Consider the horrific example of Eastern Air Lines Flight 401, bound from New York to Miami on December 29, 1972. The jumbo jet had a full load of holiday passengers as it began its final descent toward the Miami International Airport. When the crew pulled the handle to lower the landing gear, one of the lights failed to turn green.

In this case, the nose-gear light had remained off, meaning that either the nose wheel hadn't safely come down and locked into place, or that the bulb itself had burned out. The pilot radioed the control tower: "Well, ah, tower, this is Eastern 401. It looks like we're gonna have to circle; we don't have a light on our nose gear yet."

The tower directed the plane to change its approach and climb back to two thousand feet. They set the autopilot to a looping race-track pattern and turned their attention to the light. The captain and the first officer attempted to replace the bulb, but discovered that the cover had jammed. After working unsuccessfully to get it out, the engineer joined in, but likewise couldn't get the light to budge. The copilot suggested they use a handkerchief to get a better grip, but whatever they ended up trying didn't help. The engineer finally suggested pliers, but warned that if they forced it, they could end up breaking the mechanism. The crew kept at it, throwing out expletives as they struggled to get the light bulb out and replaced with another.

The cockpit voice recorder captured the second officer next,[7] "We did something to the altitude."

"What?" the captain replied, confused.

"We're still at two thousand feet, right?" the copilot asked.

The captain then uttered his last words: "Hey, what's happening here?"

The microphone captured the sounds of the airliner flying itself into the Everglades, taking the lives of 101 passengers and crew.

The final report cited pilot error as the cause of the crash, citing that "the failure of the flight crew to monitor the flight instruments during the final four minutes of flight, and to detect an unexpected descent soon enough to prevent impact with the ground. Preoccupation with a malfunction . . . distracted the crew's attention from the instruments and allowed the descent to go unnoticed."[8]

While this example is extreme, solving the problem of the landing-gear light was certainly urgent. Landing the airplane safely, however, was of paramount importance. Unfortunately, in their zeal to address the urgent, the crew got distracted and unintentionally lost sight of what mattered most.

In the workplace, urgencies tend to be easy to identify, like picking up the phone, answering a text, or clicking an email. But as the example of Flight 401 illustrates, the tendency to confuse what's urgent with what's important can have long-standing consequences. Like the next ball being served up to us by the pinball machine, it's a constant press of urgencies that act on us: They vie for our immediate intention. By contrast, important things often require us to act on them. Important things are those that contribute to our values and align to our highest goals. They are intentional and long-term rather than ad hoc and transitory. In almost all cases, they include important relationships.

The nature of the pinball syndrome is to confuse urgency with importance. And since organizations often reward urgent behaviors (because by their very nature they're easy to recognize), work can provide a powerful incentive to pull the plunger back and play round after round. Of course, urgencies will come up that require our attention. Many things are both urgent *and* important. When I talk about avoiding the pinball syndrome, I'm not advocating that we step away from the game altogether, but rather, that we differentiate between when we *must* play and when we *choose* to play. The pinball game is rigged and, in the end, will eventually have its way. Despite whatever totals we've racked up on the scoreboard, or the long hours we've devoted over nights and weekends, the ball eventually slips through. Any win is temporary at best, and we're only given a small respite before the score resets and the next ball ratchets into place. It's what we do in that moment—between reaching for the plunger and taking our hands off and stepping back—that will make all the difference. At its core, it's the same difference between the two funerals I attended: a man who played a seemingly never-ending game for the illusion of a high score, and a woman who chose to step away from the game and connect with the people standing around her. Resisting the allure of the game isn't easy. It requires that we delay gratification and take the long-term view. With that in mind, here are two suggestions that may help:

- **Set goals that matter.** Reflect on what's important to you at the deepest and most meaningful levels. Be specific. This process is how a GPS works—we need to identify a destination first to calculate which roads will get us there most directly. The more exact the address, the better the chance we'll arrive. Goals that matter are those that are typically centered on strengthening relationships, planning for the future, and personal improvement.

- **Choose your weekly priorities carefully.** Rather than just a to-do list, think about which activities will have the greatest impact on your relationships and the outcomes you care most about. Consider which actions would build trust, make work easier for people, help you be more patient in your dealings with others, or create value for your customers. Try thinking about your weekly calendar as rows of empty containers, each limited by a finite amount of space (i.e., time). People who suffer from the pinball syndrome kid themselves into believing they can fit everything in—all the numerous small and urgent tasks along with the fewer, more valuable and important ones. We tend to focus on the quick wins first, shoving as many urgent tasks into our limited containers as we can. And although the containers are full, they're not often filled with meaningful accomplishments. But here's the problem: Once these limited spaces fill up with urgencies, the important things naturally fall by the wayside. When represented in a calendar, these containers filled with urgencies look something like this:

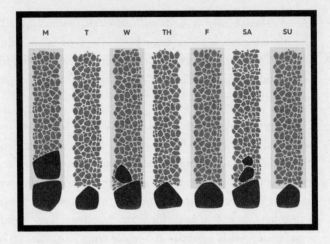

If we thoughtfully identify and schedule the most important things first (the priorities that require us to act on them rather than react to them), what falls by the wayside are the urgent, less important things. And because they're less important, we won't get derailed if they don't get done right away.

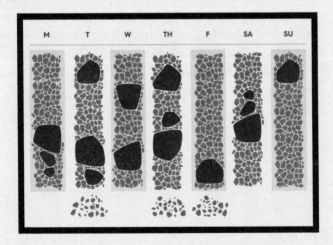

I have a reminder of the pinball syndrome enshrined in my office. Several years ago, our people-services team brainstormed ideas to improve the culture at our corporate office. At the time, people were working hard, but they didn't seem to be enjoying it much. We came up with four initiatives to focus on and captured them on my office whiteboard. We had great passion and enthusiasm for the list, but as we returned to our work, we were inundated with all the typical urgencies. We talked about the list for weeks but, after a while, we stopped noticing it altogether. Three years passed, and I still resisted the urge to wipe the list from my board—hanging on to the hope that we'd get to it sometime. It was important, after all. Eventually, I surrendered. Somewhat discouraged, I went to erase the list, only to find it wouldn't come off! Even though it had been written with a dry-erase marker, the list had been there so long that it had become permanent. Our team had fallen prey to the pinball syndrome. We became so caught up in the urgent that we didn't focus on the things that might have made the greatest impact on our culture. And now I had a permanent reminder of what that looked like.

Often urgencies show up as things, but people can pull us into the pinball syndrome as easily as a to-do list. Let me share a few strategies I've learned that can prevent us from getting sucked into people-created urgencies:

- **Block your schedule.** Purposely carve out as many blocks of time as you can each week to deal with unplanned events or crises that might surface. Let everyone around you know at the beginning of the week when you will be available. If no unexpected crises surface, you'll get the benefit of a few extra minutes to focus on the important, nonurgent things like strategic planning, relationship building, forecasting, crisis prevention, and raising teenagers.

- **Reflect on your day.** Look back over the day and ask what worked and what didn't, then make a resolution to handle things better the next day. The purpose of such reflection is to learn, not to beat yourself up over what you failed to do.

- **Be ready for drop-ins.** Rehearse language to use when people drop in with their issues and urgent requests. If I'm asked to take on a sudden new project, my response might be: "Here's my challenge. I absolutely want to be helpful. But I also want to be realistic about the commitments I've made to other people. Let me give you an idea of what I think I can realistically do." Sometimes when someone asks me if I have a minute to talk, I honestly respond, "I do have a minute, but I don't have five. Can we handle this in a minute? If not, let's schedule a time when we can give it the attention it deserves."

One of the sinister aspects of the pinball syndrome is that it can ensnare any of us, which was what I suspected was happening with Melissa . . .

• • •

"I hear you, Todd, I really do," Melissa replied as her phone gave off a ping. She glanced down at the message and I waited while she scanned it before silencing her device. "Sorry about that, but you see how busy things are. In a perfect world, I'd love to have regular one-on-one meetings with everyone on my team, I really would. But that's not my reality. Honestly, I just don't have the time."

It was a classic response from a talented and dedicated person stuck in the pinball syndrome. I could almost picture Melissa hovered over the game, doing her best to keep the ball in play, unaware that her team was surrounding her.

I reflected on my whiteboard with the now infamous unerasable list—I knew as well as anyone that it was easy to lose sight of what was important in the pinball syndrome. "Melissa, is keeping Garret on your team something that's important to you?"

"Very much so."

"Tell me more about what's going on," I asked.

"It's so disheartening to hear how Garret is feeling. I really appreciate and value him as a member of the team. And I can see how having to cancel our appointments didn't help any."

"Tell me more about that, if you don't mind? What happened?"

"Well, you know how it is at the end of the quarter. I get pretty

swamped with demands from the various departments I support. Lots of last-minute requests and things like that."

"Do you take that into account when planning your calendar? I mean, it sounds like you can pretty much predict this surge will happen at the end of every quarter."

Melissa considered it for a moment. "Well, obviously, not as much as I should."

"Tell me about your typical day," I asked.

"Well, every morning I look at my to-do list and start working through it. I usually don't get very far before something pops up. But that's just the nature of the job, so I try and get as much accomplished as possible before the day's out and then pick it back up again tomorrow."

"Okay, so given where you typically spend your time and energy, how do you think Garret would see himself in your day-to-day priorities?"

Melissa hesitated, unconsciously glancing at her phone. "Honestly, I can see how he might think he's unimportant. But that's not how I feel at all."

"I think you're probably right," I agreed. "I suppose the question is how can you change that?"

"I need to talk to him," Melissa replied.

One of the causalities of living in the pinball syndrome is losing sight of where you end up. Despite her good intentions, Melissa had missed the cues that her team was growing frustrated.

"I think that's good," I said.

"But I don't know how to solve my time issue."

"Do you mind if I make a suggestion?"

"Of course not."

"The way you describe your day, it's like you're in a never-ending battle to try and finish your to-do list."

Melissa nodded. "It does feel like that."

"It seems to be a given that you're probably always going to be leaving something undone—as you phrased it, 'to pick it back up again tomorrow.'"

"That's true."

"So maybe the question isn't so much about how you squeeze more in, but what you let go? Maybe you're allowing the urgencies to take precedence over what's really important, such as your team's need to spend more time with you."

"*I hadn't really thought of it like that,*" Melissa said, "*but maybe you're right. I could block out time for not only the end-of-quarter emergencies, but also for my team before the crises set in.*"

"*Try to build an immovable wall around the important things,*" I continued. "*It's okay if the urgent but unimportant stuff slips a little.*"

"*I guess it's hard to give yourself permission to do that—at least for me, anyway.*"

"*I think probably for all of us,*" I agreed, doing my best not to glance back at my whiteboard. When Melissa left, I felt optimistic that she was going to start resisting the allure of the pinball syndrome and invest more in her team. And I was going to request a new whiteboard.

AVOID THE PINBALL SYNDROME

1. At the end of the week, print out last week's calendar and task list or, if you don't manage those things electronically, keep a time log for one week and record the activities you participate in— preferably on an hourly basis.

2. Circle the urgent activities and underline the important activities. If you find every activity (including the urgent ones) as important, prioritize them.

3. Identify what percentage of your time you dedicate to the urgent and how much to the important.

4. Decide which one or two urgent activities you can let go of or postpone next week, then block out time on next week's calendar for one or two important things to put in their place.

THINK WE, NOT ME

DO YOU ONLY SEE YOUR ABILITY TO WIN OR SUCCEED WHEN IT COMES AT THE EXPENSE OF OTHERS? OR DO YOU TAKE CARE OF EVERYONE ELSE AT YOUR OWN EXPENSE?

If either of these is true, you may want to consider

PRACTICE 7: THINK WE, NOT ME.

When you don't "think we, not me," your room may feel like Sartre's hell because:

- You live with the fear that there's never enough, perhaps resenting others around you when they succeed.
- You achieve short-term wins at the expense of genuine, long-term successes.
- People will want to exit *your* room as fast as they can because they don't want to live or work with a martyr.

Because a major part of my job involves listening to people all day long, if I have a free moment, I may choose to eat lunch by myself for a little down time. Those who are particularly adept at squeezing in an impromptu, unscheduled meeting have been known to lie in wait and ambush me during such unguarded moments. I'm not sure that's what Lewis, a mid-forties senior manager who oversees a large sales territory for the organization, had in mind, but he was definitely making a beeline in my direction.

"Hey, Todd," he announced as he approached, sounding more anxious than enthusiastic. "I'm glad I ran into you. You have a moment?"

"Sure," I replied, realizing my alone time would need to wait.

"I appreciate it. I'm struggling with something, and I hoped I could talk it through with you."

"No problem. Do you mind if we talk while we walk?" I asked, wanting to get a little fresh air. Lewis agreed, and we started to walk around the campus. "So, what's going on?"

"We've got a compensation problem," Lewis replied. "You know I appreciate my job and that I'm well paid, but I'm struggling with the fact that one of my direct reports is going to make more than I will this year."

"Can you tell me more?" I asked.

"It just doesn't feel right. I mean, why would anyone aspire to my position if their direct reports can make more money than they do? Frankly, I don't think we should have a situation where a subordinate makes more than his or her boss. And that's what's happening with Brenda."

"You don't think Brenda's performance is up to par?" I asked. Brenda was a particularly talented salesperson who had been doing a terrific job in the territory.

"You misunderstand," Lewis corrected. "It's not about Brenda's performance—it's about the fact that she's making more than I am!"

● ● ●

We live in a competitive world—our educational, corporate, sports, and legal systems (just to name a few) encourage and reward us to one-up each other, reach the top of the bell curve, land in the uppermost percentile, score the most points, or add the definitive "W" to the win column. In one of our well-known workshops, we begin with a game to help people understand just how invested they are in winning. The facilitator introduces the game saying something like this: "Most kids love to play Tic-Tac-Toe. Was that true for you?" Usually everyone nods in agreement. The facilitator then asks the participants, "So, what was the point of the game when you played it as a child?"

"To win as fast and as often as you could!" most program participants respond.

At that point, the facilitator asks people to pair up and play a few rounds of a new game, saying, "So the game we're going to play isn't exactly Tic-Tac-Toe, but something very similar called *Extreme Tic-Tac-Toe*. Every *four* items in a row achieved (x's or o's), yields one point. If you finish the first game during the allotted time, immediately start a new game. Remember, the goal is to *win as fast and as much as you can!*"

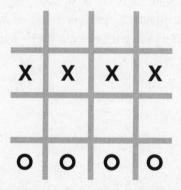

The first round often ignites the competitive win conditioning many of us grew up learning. Individuals start to pit themselves against one another, working furiously to beat their partner by increasing their individual score. At the end of Round One, each pair shares the total points they achieved. Most pairs get only a few points, since they have been competing.

The facilitator then gives each pair time to strategize before the second round, emphasizing that the goal is to *win as fast and as much as you can*. Gradually, the partnerships begin to realize they don't have to fight each other for points. Rather, they can work together to accumulate points. They see that they can work faster and more efficiently cooperating instead of competing. Once they have this "aha" moment, they start to fill up their game cards as fast as possible. After the second or third round of the game, the partners get four, six, or even ten times the number of points they did working alone.

As human beings, we've been conditioned to view the world as having only so much to offer, so we'd better get *ours* while we can. I remember a colleague once sharing with me how difficult the holiday season was for him as a child. When I inquired as to why, he answered, "Because as I watched my siblings retrieve their presents, I thought to myself, *Well, there's one less for me.* And I had a lot of siblings!"

THE IMPORTANCE OF MINDSETS

For my colleague (and for many of us), we resign ourselves to live with a win-lose mentality: If you get a present, I don't. There are several other mindsets when it comes to how we live and work with others:

- Lose-win
- Lose-lose
- Win-lose
- Win-win

These mindsets are largely driven by two factors:

- The nature of our maturity level.
- The amount of courage and consideration we employ when dealing with others.

LEVELS OF MATURITY

At FranklinCovey, we teach about three levels of maturity: dependence, independence, and interdependence. Dependence comes with the mindset of "you." *You* are responsible for me, for my feelings and circumstances. It's *your* job to take care of me. We all experienced this level of maturity when we came into this world. As infants, we were dependent on our caregivers for everything: food, clothing, shelter, and love. There's nothing wrong with being dependent in certain situations. But how many of us have worked with adults who are still stuck in dependent behavior: They believe that you or others are responsible for their successes and failures, their moods and feelings. Dependence represents the lowest level of personal maturity, where we can consign our happiness to others or adopt a victim mentality when things go wrong. It often sounds like *you* let me down, *you* make me so mad, *you* didn't come through, it's *your* fault.

However, when we take on a new role or skill, there is a period of time during which it's expected that we'll be dependent on others to teach us as we learn that new skill. Many years ago when I first became a physician recruiter in the medical industry, I had no training in the field. I was reliant on other professional recruiters to learn the ropes. You could say I was dependent on them. But little by little, I learned and grew in maturity.

Independence, the next level of maturity, comes with the mindset of "I." Independence sounds like *I* am the one who can do this, *I* am responsible, *I* will decide what's best. When we think and act at this level, we move our focus from the people around us to our own strengths and capabilities. For many of us, we think independence is the pinnacle of maturity. Once I had a few years' experience building my knowledge and skills as a physician recruiter, I began to see myself as highly successful. I thought I had arrived. What more was there to learn? (See "Practice 15: Start With Humility.")

While independence is certainly more mature than dependence, there's something even more satisfying and transformational that happens when independent people choose to work together.

With interdependence, we adopt the mindset of "*we*." When we think and act interdependently—we make a choice to combine our talents and capabilities with those of others, creating something even greater as a result. Interdependence sounds like together *we* can do it, together *we* can collaborate, and together *we* can figure this out. I remember attending my first industry convention where I met other successful professionals who had been in the business far longer than I had been. It was then that I came off my big independent throne and realized just how much I had to learn from others.

Many studies seem to suggest that nature uses cooperative strategies and not just survival of the fittest. There's something innately powerful about cooperation, about banding together and leveraging each other's strengths.

The most effective way to strengthen our relationships and find win-win is by seeing and adopting the mindset of interdependence. If we're not careful, when we're in situations that can trigger reactivity, we can drop to independent, or worse, dependent behavior—blaming and accusing others or holding others responsible for our emotional well-being. Here's how *not* having an interdependent mindset played out for me.

Some years ago, a colleague completely rewrote an important presentation I had prepared. When I looked at the changes, negative thoughts came flooding in: *Who does she think she is? I've been doing this for years, and suddenly she's the expert? Maybe she should just do the entire thing herself!* I assumed bad intent, questioned her motives, and fell into a victim mentality. I was focusing on how *she* made *me* mad—living in a state of dependence. I had allowed the situation to become a competition between me and my colleague.

Later, I began to feel even more defiant: *I've received plenty of accolades, and I don't need anyone else's feedback. I know what I'm doing. I just need to press forward and forget about her.* I had slipped into the independent level of maturity, seeing my colleague as an obstacle standing in the way. I was prepared to double down on my own capabilities and dismiss her feedback altogether.

But the next day, I shared what was happening with a trusted friend. He listened patiently as I ran through my own plans and litany of complaints. When I was done, he replied, "I can imagine how difficult it would be to hear criticism about your performance after all the work you've done. I also want you to know that your ability to engage an audience is one of the primary reasons you're asked to deliver these presentations. You're good at what you do, Todd."

His sincerity started to soften the defensiveness I was feeling. He continued, "Putting aside the somewhat abrasive way she chose to share her feedback, I actually believe some of her comments would make your presentation better. It might be helpful for you to separate how you're feeling about the feedback from some of her potentially useful suggestions. I can tell she wants you to emphasize a few key points because it will make the presentation more persuasive. Her idea to start the presentation with the inspirational quote will help the audience understand the concept faster." He shared a few other points I was unable to hear the day before.

He got me thinking, *Was it possible she wanted to help make my presentation the best it could be? Certainly, she had a vested interest in the outcome. Perhaps there was more to be gained by working together rather than separately . . .*

My friend's wise coaching allowed me to put my defensiveness aside and genuinely consider the feedback. He concluded, "I honestly believe her heart is in the right place. Her technique may not be that great, but her intent is unquestionable—she wants to help."

With an interdependent mindset, my friend helped me push my ego aside and dive into what my colleague had suggested and why. While I didn't accept every suggestion, I came to realize that many of her recommendations made the presentation stronger. I even asked for another meeting with her to rehearse what I'd learned. I chose to work interdependently. When it came time to deliver the presentation again, it was much improved. Since then, I've asked for her advice on other presentations I've been tasked to prepare and deliver.

COURAGE AND CONSIDERATION

Those who consistently model interdependence balance courage and consideration when working with others. We define *courage* as the willingness and ability to speak our thoughts respectfully, and *consideration* as our willingness and ability to seek and listen to others' thoughts and feelings with respect. While it's challenging to maintain a perfect balance of both in every situation, the real thing to look for is to make sure you're not dramatically weighted toward one side or the other. Too much consideration without enough courage can turn you into a so-called pushover or doormat. Too much courage without enough consideration can turn you into a bully.

Too Much Courage

Years ago I worked with a man whose reputation preceded him. He had a rough exterior, a short temper, and interrupted people constantly. When he disagreed with something or shared feedback with others, he gave no thought as to how his offensive style would make them feel. You can imagine how excited I was when I was assigned to work with him on a critical project.

As we started to orchestrate the team, every person I recommended was immediately shot down by him: "He's an idiot." "She doesn't have any clout." "He's not right for the job." And so on. Lacking courage wasn't his issue. The following six months of the project were the longest in my life. Surprisingly, we finished the project on time, but no one wanted to work with him again. And he continued as a lone genius for the rest of his career.

Too Much Consideration

In a previous career, I worked with a person who had nothing *but* consideration. He would run other people's errands on his lunch hour, always worked long hours, and volunteered to do others' assignments on the weekends, even tasks that were outside of his job description or areas of responsibility. Sensitive to any negative feedback, he avoided saying no to anyone. While he was well liked (who *wouldn't* like him, he never said no!), he lacked the courage to speak his opinions with confidence and told me he didn't always feel respected. Over the years he became exhausted, demoralized, and felt underappreciated by everyone.

While great ideas and high courage can be critical to doing a job well, without consideration and respect, the only team you will find yourself on is a team of one. On the other hand, with high consideration but no courage, you may be well liked but will ultimately feel disrespected. Like the highly courageous person who alienates others, the highly considerate person may also feel alone.

The challenge is to demonstrate high courage and high consideration equally across *all* relationships. Sometimes we're more courageous at home than we are at work, or more considerate with our professional colleagues than we are with our personal relationships. When we strive to balance both equally, we pave the way to interdependence and mutually beneficial outcomes in all relationships. How we choose to view and work with others leads to one of four outcomes. Let me illustrate by using the story I shared earlier—the one in which I felt my colleague was rewriting my presentation.

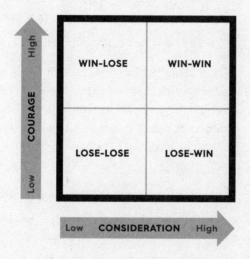

- Lose-win (high consideration, low courage). I concede that my colleague is right in rewriting the presentation and that I'm wrong for questioning her. I capitulate to her thinking and accept her changes universally, taking the path of least resistance.

  - What lose-win looks like:

    - I lack courage to express or ask for what I need.

- I'm often intimidated—I give in easily.

- I'm motivated by acceptance from others.

- I tend to hide my true feelings about things.

- Lose-lose (low consideration, low courage). Feeling attacked and belittled, I'm completely justified in trashing the entire presentation—her version and mine. Not only am I *not* interested in what my colleague says, but I'm willing to abandon my work as well. Somebody else can waste time on it if he or she wants to, but I'm through. And too bad if she can't find a replacement at this late date.

  - What lose-lose looks like:

    - If I'm going to lose, so are you.

    - I'm willing to be hurt, so long as you are too.

    - I give up on what's really important.

- Win-lose (high courage, low consideration). Since my colleague fired the first shot and attacked me, I'm perfectly justified in doing the same. I'll just hit "reject all" on her revisions, then craft a lengthy email and give her a piece of my mind. She needs to be put in her place.

  - What win-lose looks like:

    - I use position, power, credentials, possessions, or personality to get my way.

    - I put down others so I look better.

    - I compete rather than collaborate.

    - I'm going to win and you're going to lose.

- Win-win (high courage and high consideration). I'm going to considerately and respectfully listen to my colleague's point of view and courteously share my own view, assuming good intent. I'll make the choice to work together, knowing we both have strengths to contribute and that we'll achieve a better outcome as a result.

- What win-win looks like:
  - We work together until we find a solution that benefits both of us.
  - I value your needs and desires equally to my own.
  - I collaborate rather than compete.
  - I balance courage and consideration when communicating.
  - I can disagree respectfully.

In my experience, the long-term impact of any outcome other than win-win will sooner or later be headed toward lose-lose.

There's tremendous power in thinking *we*, not *me*. Not only are we more likely to achieve the results we want, but we strengthen relationships along the way—something I wondered if Lewis, the senior manager who was concerned over the compensation of one of his direct reports, had lost sight of.

● ● ●

"You misunderstand," Lewis corrected. "It's not about Brenda's performance—it's about the fact that she's making more than I am!"

"It sounds like you're seeing this as a competition," I replied as we continued our walk, "that the winner here is the person who ends up making the most money."

Lewis considered that for a moment before replying. "I think it's about fairness, not about a competition."

"Okay, let's go with that then," I continued. "Don't you benefit when Brenda performs well?"

"Sure," Lewis answered. "I mean, I own the number for the entire area and her contribution helps me hit my target."

"So you make more when Brenda performs well and you more easily hit your goals—maybe even sleep a little easier at night knowing that particular part of the region is performing."

"Yeah," Lewis admitted.

"And meanwhile, Brenda continues to be motivated to work hard and grow the region even more. Let's say we restructure the compensation plan in your area to keep Brenda from performing past a certain ceiling. How do you think she'd respond to that?"

"Well, she of course wouldn't like it," Lewis replied. "She'd probably be tempted to coast once she hit the cap."

"Would she be frustrated enough to move elsewhere?" I asked.

"I hope not, but you never know. I guess she might start looking."

I paused and stared at Lewis. "And how is that good for you? To me, it sounds like a lose-lose. You may make a point about compensation, but in the end, it would hurt both of you. Is that really what you want?"

Lewis sighed. "No. It's just the principle of the thing."

"You know there are two other senior sales managers who have team members making more than they are making, right? They actually revel in the fact that they have the kind of people working for them who can earn so much. The truth is, if Brenda happens to take a bigger slice of the pie, she's not taking it off your plate; she's made the entire pie bigger for everyone. That seems like a win-win to me."

"Maybe," Lewis admitted.

I continued, "You've been a good leader. You've mentored her over the years and helped her get where she is. That's worth something. Is money the only way to calculate success?"

"I guess not," Lewis said.

"One option would be for you to go back to a pure sales role. You'd probably make more money as a result. But that would mean giving up leading your team—which you're great at, by the way, and something I think really matters to you."

"No, you're right. I don't want to give that up. Maybe I'm losing sight of the other rewards besides just money."

"Why not mentor each salesperson on your team to the point where they become so successful that their compensation passes yours."

Lewis nodded. "I'll have to think about that."

While Lewis continued to struggle with Brenda's pay, I've seen other leaders take great pride in watching their team members' financial successes model the spirit of think we, not me.

THINK WE, NOT ME

When you exercise a balance of high courage and high consideration in your relationships, you're well on your way to thinking "we," not "me." To get better at this practice, complete the following exercise.

---

1. Pick one personal and one professional relationship that is currently strained or less than ideal.

2. Rate the level of courage and consideration you show in each relationship, then place the name of the person where it fits on the grid. (See the example that follows.)

3. Where you place each name on the grid determines how you typically interact with that person. If you are low on consideration and high on courage in one relationship, you may be acting in a win-lose way. If you're high on consideration and low on courage in a different relationship, you might be acting in a lose-win way.

4. Remember, the ideal is to have a high level of both courage and consideration in all relationships—personal and professional.

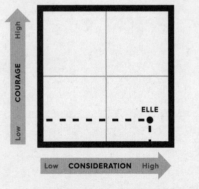

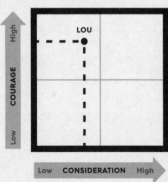

5. If you find you're low on courage, try the following:

   • Write out your ideas and opinions, and practice articulating them with a few safe people.

- Practice asking for things. Start with things you are sure you'll get.

- Commit to contribute one idea in your next meeting.

- Follow up conversations with a written version of your comments.

6. If you're low on consideration, try these ideas (but be sensitive to how distinctive cultural norms may require a different approach):

   - Turn off all devices and make eye contact when talking with people.

   - In meetings, wait to speak until two or three people have shared their ideas.

   - Don't interrupt.

   - Jot down your ideas to remember rather than articulating them in the moment, especially when emotions are high.

   - Finish your idea with a question, asking for input from others.

TAKE STOCK OF YOUR EMOTIONAL BANK ACCOUNTS

ARE YOU AT RISK OF BEING OVERDRAWN OR EVEN BANKRUPT IN ANY OF YOUR RELATIONSHIPS?

If so, you may want to consider

PRACTICE 8: TAKE STOCK OF YOUR EMOTIONAL BANK ACCOUNTS.

When you don't take stock of your Emotional Bank Accounts, your room may feel like Sartre's hell because:

- You're confused as to why someone doesn't appreciate your attempts to be helpful.
- Recovering from a mistake takes far longer than it should.
- You inadvertently lose the trust of important relationships around you.

I looked down at my buzzing phone and saw the name Jerome pop up, an old friend I hadn't talked to in years. We'd worked closely together at a previous company but had managed to lose touch. I was delighted to hear his voice when I answered.

"Todd, it's been too long," Jerome announced, his voice as big and cheerful as ever.

"I know. It's great to hear from you."

"I've been thinking about you and your family and just wanted to say hi."

We reminisced about our old organization and where our lives had taken us. After a few minutes, Jerome expressed his regret we hadn't connected sooner. "It was great to get caught up," he added. "You know, we should go to lunch sometime." I agreed and told him I'd get back in touch. I was just about to thank him again for the call when he interjected, "Oh, you know what I just remembered? Does your uncle still get those discount tickets for the Friends and Family Day at the Sports Hut?"

I was a little taken aback. Suddenly, all the good feelings I'd had about reconnecting with my old colleague were replaced with the suspicion that his unexpected call had more to do with my uncle and his discount tickets than with me.

"I'm not sure. I'll have to check," I answered in a somewhat monotone voice.

I then excused myself and hung up. "Wow," I thought. "What an opportunist." Usually, I would have been happy to ask my uncle for a favor, but not now.

• • •

Most of us pay a good deal of attention to our financial bank accounts—the deposits and withdrawals, the interest and penalties, the opening and closing balances on our statements. The idea is fairly straightforward: We deposit funds in order to build up a reservoir from which our various future expenses are withdrawn. Today's technology allows us to monitor these transactions in nearly real time. When it comes to our relationships, we engage in similar kinds of transactions, either making deposits or withdrawals in what we at FranklinCovey call the *Emotional Bank Account (EBA)*. When the balance is high, so is the resulting level of trust. When the balance is low, relationships suffer. While there are many similarities between the way a traditional bank account and an Emotional Bank Account operates, there are a few key differences worth noting:

- **The goal of the EBA is to only make deposits and build trust with others.** We never accumulate a balance in order to make purposeful, planned withdrawals at a later time.

- **Emotional Bank Accounts don't allow for automated deposits.** Unlike your regular bank account, you can't sign up for recurring direct deposits (like payroll) with your EBA. Deposits in the Emotional Bank Account require us to walk up to the teller, as it were, and make the transaction in person. This attention is important, because it's been my experience that it's usually the relationships we take for granted—the ones on autopilot—that are most in need of consistent and deliberate attention.

- **High trust, good will, and full engagement are the ultimate outcome of the EBA,** not high monetary yields or robust interest accruals. When you have a high EBA balance with someone, you feel safe and energized. If you're wondering what your account balance with a particular person might be, consider how you react when they call: do you answer their call once you see their name on the caller ID, or even if you have the time available, do you let it go to voicemail? When they show up unexpectedly at your door, is your first instinct to welcome them in, or to duck behind the sofa when you see them coming? When they ask for a favor, are you eager to help and say yes before even knowing what the favor is, or are you dreading the request? Every relationship we have has an associated balance in our respective Emotional Bank Accounts. Consider some of the ways we make deposits and withdrawals:

DEPOSIT	WITHDRAWAL
Seek first to understand.	Assume you understand.
Show kindness, courtesy, and respect.	Show cruelty, impoliteness, and contempt.
Keep promises.	Break promises or make no promises at all.
Be loyal to the absent.	Be untrustworthy and disloyal when people aren't around; bad-mouth or gossip.
Set clear expectations.	Create ambiguous expectations or none at all.
Apologize.	Be remorseless, proud, and arrogant.
Give feedback.	Stay silent or give feedback with bad intent.
Forgive.	Hold grudges.

You've likely heard of the tried-and-true best practices for building wealth, such as making a budget, deciding on priorities, recording expenses, etc. Similarly, here are six best practices for building a strong, high EBA balance:

1. Never deposit to withdraw.
2. Know the other person's currency.
3. Communicate your own currency.
4. Avoid counterfeit deposits.
5. Make small, consistent deposits over time.
6. Right wrongs.

NEVER DEPOSIT TO WITHDRAW

In Sartre's fictional hell, it's only through a sincere and honest focus on others that we can turn the afterlife's prison into paradise. To that end, we should never build up deposits just so we can withdraw from them when it's useful. I know a colleague who kept a box of thank-you notes in his office because he'd developed an unhealthy habit of using them to build a reservoir of goodwill before dumping a big project on someone. This approach is exactly how *not* to utilize the Emotional Bank Account.

Manipulations, or using the EBA as a means to an end, may damage relationships beyond repair. If the withdrawal is egregious and the Emotional Bank Account is low, you may have to make numerous deposits to rebuild the relationship and reestablish trust, or worst case, the withdrawal may bankrupt the account forever. In contrast, if the withdrawal is minor and the account is high, a few sincere deposits can bring it back into balance. Keep in mind that every relationship is different. If you're keeping score, you're missing the point. Striving for a high balance in an Emotional Bank Account is a principle to live by, not a scorecard.

KNOW THE OTHER PERSON'S CURRENCY

All bank accounts require their approved form of currency. It might be tempting, after a particularly successful game of Monopoly, to take your newly acquired stack of money and deposit it into your actual bank account. (Warning: You might go directly to jail.) Despite the validity of the colorful currency used in the Monopoly game, your bank is going to have different thoughts on the matter. So, too, with people—we all have individual forms of currency we're willing to accept. In life, what amounts to a deposit for one person can be meaningless or even a withdrawal for another. This unanticipated withdrawal is what happened with a friend of mine named Leslie.

Leslie decided to take the day off to go snow-skiing with her younger sister, Kristen. While not an expert skier, Leslie had more experience than her sibling, who wanted to graduate from the beginner's snowplow to more advanced techniques. As the two sisters hit the slopes, Kristen immediately struggled. Each time the younger sibling tried to transition out of the snowplow, she picked up speed, lost her balance, and fell. After completing several runs on the more advanced hills, Leslie decided to ski over and help her sister out. Having gone through the same sort of learning herself, Leslie began offering her younger sister pointers: *Lean back a little more, bend your knees, put your weight on your downhill ski, and so on.*

With each failed attempt, Leslie offered more advice to her sister, who was growing more and more frustrated as time went on. Finally, Kristen threw her poles down and exclaimed, "If I want your advice, I'll ask for it!"

Leslie was taken aback. She remembered her own struggles as a novice and appreciated the helpful tips offered by the more experienced skiers. But then again, Kristen wasn't Leslie—Kristen was more competitive than her older sister and always had a hard time when she wasn't good at something right off the bat. In effect, what had been currency for Leslie wasn't the same for Kristen. What was meant to be a deposit had ended up being a withdrawal.

I had a similar experience with emotional currency many years ago. I was in a management meeting when the finance team presented a new spreadsheet. I didn't have a clue as to how to read it. From my perspective, it was completely unintelligible—kind of like opera. The problem was, everyone but me seemed to understand it just fine. So I sat there mute, feeling stupid. I did my best to put on a sage look, staring intently at the report, and nodding my head when I noticed others doing the same. After a long discussion, one of the members of the team turned to me and asked for my opinion.

"Well," I said after a long pause. "I think the numbers speak for themselves." I smiled, and people around the table laughed. I hoped my subtle humor would hide the fact that if the numbers were speaking, it was a foreign language to me. I managed to deflect the question, and the meeting continued. Afterward, one of the team members pulled me aside.

"I really enjoy your sense of humor, Todd," he said. "May I ask you something?

"Sure," I said.

"You seemed a little uncomfortable with the new financial report. Can I help?"

"Actually, yes," I answered. "How about a time machine so I can retake all the accounting classes I failed in college?"

He smiled warmly. "Can't help you there, but I could walk you through the report. I don't think it's as complicated as it may look." Such an offer could have made me feel insecure, but it didn't. My colleague recognized that I used humor as a way of deflecting my anxiety, and let me know he both appreciated it and understood why I felt the need to go there. He sensed that I was a little uncomfortable, and rather than speak about it in front of the others, offered to do so in private. He understood a currency important to me (and to most people I know) of not being put on the spot in public. He built trust and made it safe to tackle what could have been a potentially embarrassing topic, making a deposit instead of a withdrawal. It didn't require a grand gesture or planning on his part; he simply recognized and used a currency important to me in building an Emotional Bank Account.

COMMUNICATE YOUR OWN CURRENCY

Admittedly, it can be hard sometimes to uncover which currency matters most to people—especially when we don't know them very well. We can help by simply communicating the currency we prefer. I learned this lesson the hard way over a sixteen-year struggle with a pineapple-based dessert. It all started when my wife and I were first married, and her aunt made a pineapple cake with whipped-cream frosting for a family party. It was one of many cakes served at the event, and I made a big deal about it when it was unveiled.

"This looks great, Aunt Gladys," I announced. "How did you know it was my favorite?" My wife, Trish, overhearing me, took note. When my birthday came, she ended up making the exact same pineapple cake, whipped-cream frosting and all. I thanked her, a little surprised to see it again, but went on to celebrate the day as planned. The following year the cake made another appearance, just like the previous year. And the tradition continued: the year after that, and the year after that. My wife ended up making the pineapple and whipped-cream frosting cake on my birthday for fifteen years. It took me that long to finally come clean.

"You know what, Trish?" I asked as my next birthday approached. "Can I admit something to you?" Perhaps this opener isn't the best open-ended question to leave lingering with a spouse, so I decided to press on. "I don't really love pineapple cake."

"You don't? Since when?"

"Well, since forever."

"But I've been making it for you all these years. I remember you telling Aunt Gladys it was your favorite."

"You're right. But it was the party where everyone brought desserts, and I noticed that nobody was eating hers. We were newly married, and I wanted to make a good impression. I didn't want her to feel bad, so I took a big slice and said it was my favorite. Seemed like a good idea at the time."

"But it wasn't your favorite?" my wife asked.

"Uh, no."

"So all this time . . ."

"I know. I'm sorry."

It took my wife some time to get over her understandably confused and hurt feelings. For fifteen years, she believed she'd been making me my favorite cake. Was it her responsibility to read my mind? Of course not. I could have (and should have) avoided hurting and confusing her many years earlier by graciously sharing that pineapple cake wasn't at the top of my list. In this situation, it was my responsibility to share with her my currency, and having to pretend I liked pineapple cake was making unnecessary EBA withdrawals. Again, that responsibility rested primarily with me—I should have simply let her know.

Too often we assume others should have special insight into what amounts to deposits and withdrawals. In fact, if we aren't careful, we can even start accusing people of making a withdrawal when their intent has been just the opposite. With just a little proactivity on our part, we can be responsible for letting people know in advance what our particular currency happens to be.

It's not only a good idea to communicate currency in our personal lives, but it's effective in our professional lives as well. We recently hired a new sales manager, Rebecca, to replace a manager who was retiring. The previous manager was very involved at the beginning of new client relationships, accompanying salespeople on their calls so that he could mentor them in how to grow existing accounts. His salespeople learned his currency: that when he was in town, they should line up as many meetings with existing accounts as they could. In contrast, Rebecca had a skill of finding and growing new business. Knowing that her salespeople had learned the old manager's currency, Rebecca met with her new team members early on to express her unique preferences. While she also wanted them to grow existing business, she preferred spending her time accompanying them on appointments with new clients. Her currency was to have them research new business and set up as many appointments with new clients as possible. Because she shared her currency early on, her salespeople didn't waste time guessing what mattered to her or trying to learn her style; they were immediately set up to succeed.

AVOID COUNTERFEIT DEPOSITS

Sometimes we make counterfeit deposits. We all know what counterfeit money is, and it's the last thing any of us wants in our bank account. Such bogus deposits can attempt to make their way into the Emotional Bank Account if we're not careful. They often take the form of contrived compliments, fake apologies, or even overly extravagant gifts. (Some might see my compliment to Aunt Gladys about her cake as contrived, but when the recipient is a ninety-year-old woman, you get cut a little slack.) Perhaps you've experienced the manager who goes from office to office telling each co-worker in vague, hyperbolic ways how fantastically wonderful they are, and how deeply and unabashedly he or she admires them. But the compliments soon feel like attempts at flattery, designed to get people to do what the manager wants them to do. Such verbal tributes become so routine and anticipated, team members begin to joke about them behind the manager's back: "Are they running for political office, or what?" All the while, EBA balances slowly diminish.

We pay a price for making counterfeit deposits into Emotional Bank Accounts. Not that you should withhold compliments when they're due—there are numerous people who do incredible work every day—but overdone flattery will never yield EBA deposits. One safeguard is to always be conscious of your intent: Are you looking for a payoff—for a return on your investment—or are you acting from a genuine concern for the person? (For more information on this question, see "Practice 9: Examine Your Real Motives.") There's a difference between a quid pro quo strategy and making an authentic deposit.

I'm again reminded of my leader and mentor, Pam, with whom I worked early on in my HR career. In "Practice 5: See the Tree, Not Just the Seedling," I told the story of how I had only been on the job thirty-five days when Pam introduced me to one of the executives and recounted what I had accomplished in my short time there. Pam could have easily said, "He's doing a really good job." But instead, she listed very specific comments about what I'd accomplished. I knew this approach wasn't artificial flattery, but that she understood and meant every word.

Along the same lines, a colleague of mine was asked to deliver a full-day workshop for a group of salespeople she didn't know very well. It was extremely challenging, to say the least. Afterward, she got a personal handwritten note that arrived at her home from our CEO, thanking her for her time. He specifically referred to a story she told that was customized to the needs of the group. He mentioned how much he appreciated her handling of two specific questions that, if not addressed appropriately, would have led the discussion in a negative direction. He also thanked her for graciously handling some of the stronger personalities in the classroom. She was completely surprised at his attention to detail and that he'd taken time to even write the note. This personal gesture was a sincere and meaningful deposit into her EBA.

MAKE SMALL, CONSISTENT
DEPOSITS OVER TIME

When we make deposits into an EBA, it requires that we're deliberate and consistent. Relationships grow in security and trust when they are built with intentional, meaningful, ongoing contributions rather than the occasional grand gesture. Many people get so good at consistently making small deposits that doing so becomes a part of who they are. This stockpile of good can be invaluable when we go through the inevitable trials life presents.

If anyone understands this principle, it's Maisie Devore. While the following story illustrates deposits of actual money, think about it in terms of how small deposits over time can result in a rich and rewarding outcome. As a young mother living in the small, rural town of Eskridge, Kansas, she wanted her children to have a community swimming pool to help fill the long summer days. However, the town didn't have the funds to build or maintain something like that; it seemed as if her desire would end up unfulfilled. But Maisie was determined to make it happen. So she began collecting cans, crushing them in her garage, and saving the money she collected.

She started walking the roads around her home, collecting cans each evening and driving them down to the recycling center. All the while, the city told her she'd never raise enough money to build and support a pool. Maisie was undeterred, and continued collecting cans, scrap metal, old car batteries, and junk from area residents. For a while, she carried the nickname of Crazy Maisie, but she persisted, one can at a time, toward her goal.

Thirty years later, she had saved over one hundred thousand dollars. The story inspired her local senator, who found grant money to cover the remaining costs, and the school board donated the land. In 2001, the pool was built across from Maisie's house, where she was able to watch her great-grandchildren swim. In time, the highway where Maisie began collecting cans was renamed in her honor. Her story provides an important reminder about the power of making small deposits over time. Is Maisie unique? I think there are people who jump at the chance to help others because they've made it a habit. If you feel the satisfaction that comes from making deposits in the Emotional Bank Accounts of others, you'll make more and more, until it becomes a pattern of living for you—much like Maisie, who ended up making a significant difference in her community, one deposit at a time.

RIGHT WRONGS

Dr. Covey shared a bit of Eastern wisdom in his teaching: *If you're going to bow, bow low.* He taught that sincere apologies make deposits into the EBA of others.

I remember Francis, a colleague of mine who was known for having a somewhat short fuse. One day he was under a serious deadline and needed to keep his production line running. The manager of another division asked him to stop the line temporarily so she could examine one of the products. He refused to stop, but she insisted.

He lost it and blew up at her. He told her where to go and how to get there, and in a voice so loud that everyone around could hear it. In our company (and hopefully yours), that kind of behavior is unacceptable. Francis knew it, and later confessed to me that he'd felt bad about what he'd done and wasn't sure what to do about it. He also admitted that, at the same time, he felt somewhat justified in his behavior. Even though he crossed an etiquette line or two, he was still serving the needs of the larger project. It was his job to make his goals, after all, and how was he supposed to do that if other people were slowing him down? Sure, he'd hurt the other manager's feelings, but didn't his own feelings and responsibilities matter too?

Over the following weekend, he was so restless he couldn't sleep. After a lot of internal debate, he decided he needed to apologize to his co-worker. On Monday morning he went straight to her office, knocked on the door, and was invited in. He apologized for raising his voice and using the kind of language that would have made anyone blush, but he hoped she would understand that he was still right, even though he'd handled it poorly. It wasn't his fault, after all, that the organization put so much pressure on the production line. Nor was it his fault that he was ultimately accountable for meeting his goals, regardless of people's hurt feelings. He continued making excuses masquerading as an apology. As you can imagine, the apology fell flat. Instead of starting down the path of righting the wrong, he doubled down and made an additional withdrawal from an already nearly bankrupt account.

The particulars of that day have faded from memory for most, and numerous reviews and quarterly goals have come and gone. But the damage done that day remains. Francis has never fully recovered from the initial withdrawal. Unfortunately, by missing the opportunity to right the wrong when it first happened, the relationship still suffers from a lack of trust.

Sincere apologies, by contrast, make deposits in the Emotional Bank Accounts of others. It is the first step in righting wrongs, but if mishandled or delayed, can cause even greater withdrawals.

By applying the six best practices for building Emotional Bank Accounts, we not only begin to develop habits out of the meaningful deposits we make to others, but we build the kind of security and trust that can weather the mistakes of unintentional withdrawals. Sartre's vision of a miserable afterlife only happens when the people in the room are actively destroying others rather than building each other up. When our energy and focus turn to consistently making EBA deposits, eternity feels a lot more like heaven than Sartre's hell.

When it came to the surprise call from my former colleague, Jerome, his request felt a little bit like the latter . . .

• • •

"Oh, you know what I just remembered? Does your uncle still get those discount tickets for the Friends and Family Day at the Sports Hut?"

I was a little taken aback. Suddenly, all the good feelings I'd had about reconnecting with my old colleague were replaced with the suspicion that his unexpected call had more to do with my uncle and his discount tickets than with me.

"*I'm not sure. I'll have to check,*" *I answered in a somewhat monotone voice.*

I then excused myself and hung up. "*Wow,*" *I thought.* "*What an opportunist.*" *Usually, I would have been happy to ask my uncle for a favor, but not now.*

Over the next few weeks, I forgot about Jerome's request. I'll admit that this favor wasn't a priority for me, probably given the unexpected EBA withdrawal I'd experienced. It fell off my radar, and I suspected Jerome felt too awkward to call me again. The experience made me take stock of the other relationships in my life and to question whether I was making conscientious and consistent deposits—especially when our most trusted and long-standing relationships can be the easiest to take for granted.

TAKE STOCK OF YOUR EMOTIONAL BANK ACCOUNTS

1. Identify an important relationship.

2. What is their "currency"? If you don't know, find out!

3. Write down three things you have not yet done for this person but you know would be deposits for him or her. Determine when and how you will make those deposits.

   1. What: _____ When: _____ How: _____

   2. What: _____ When: _____ How: _____

   3. What: _____ When: _____ How: _____

4. Write down three things you have done in the past that may have been unintentional withdrawals, which you haven't yet repaired. Identify how you will make amends, if necessary, and how you will avoid these withdrawals in the future.

   1. _____

   2. _____

   3. _____

EXAMINE YOUR REAL MOTIVES

ARE YOUR MOTIVES ALIGNED WITH YOUR VALUES AND ACTIONS? DO YOU EVEN KNOW WHAT YOUR UNDERLYING MOTIVES ARE?

If not, you may want to consider

PRACTICE 9: EXAMINE YOUR REAL MOTIVES.

When you don't examine your real motives, your room may feel like Sartre's hell because:

- You get hijacked by unconscious behaviors that lead to ineffective outcomes.
- You may think you're fooling others when you're not—your motives speak louder than your words or actions.
- You start to lose sight of your values and who you really want to be.

Kevin read the companywide email with disappointment. There it was, the entire technology strategy he'd spent months crafting. He had checked and double-checked the research, studied the market analysis until he'd practically memorized it, and spent long hours going back and forth with various vendors to identify the right partner. He had given it to Sam, his boss, in a written plan. Sam praised his work as insightful and original, offering a few suggestions here and there, but mostly accepting the entire proposal as written.

"This is terrific work. You're a great talent," Sam shared with Kevin, who appreciated the compliment. It had been a tremendous amount of work, but it was worth it.

Or at least that's what he thought until he read the companywide email.

Sam had announced in the email several upcoming technology initiatives, which included a cut-and-paste copy of Kevin's plan. But what it didn't include was any indication that Kevin was the one who'd created it. And although Sam didn't explicitly take credit for the plan himself, the email implied Sam was responsible for it. Suddenly, all the satisfaction Kevin felt from his weeks of hard work turned to resentment. "Why does Sam always do this?"

Kevin sent an email to Sam, requesting a breakfast meeting for the next morning, which Sam accepted. "Maybe I'll tell him I quit," he thought to himself. "At the very least, I'm going to let him know I'm tired of him taking credit for everyone's work. What is he thinking?"

● ● ●

Motives are the underlying reasons for the actions you take and the words you say. There are healthy and unhealthy motives, as we'll explore later in this section. No one can tell you what your motives are. They may try, but you are the only one who can know your reasons for doing what you do.

Imagine if we treated motives like flying a plane. The pilot has moments of hands-on, intentional action, but most of the flying occurs with the autopilot on—upward of 90 percent. Putting the plane into autopilot allows the pilot to focus on other things such as navigation, communication, and systems operation. When it comes to people, however, there's great risk in allowing our motives to simply run unchecked in the background.

Recently my friend Jerry told me his story. Jerry had been promoted to a senior leadership position years ago. While he was excited about the job, like all of us, he had some self-doubts. *Am I ready for this role? Will I make a mistake that makes me look bad? Will others respect me if I fail?*

Jerry's boss, a wise man, pulled him aside and gave him some very specific advice: "While it's important to look good and achieve your revenue goals, years from now no one is going to remember if you made your exact numbers," he said. "The legacy you leave to your people—how you help them grow and how you allow them to make mistakes *while* they grow—is what counts and what they'll remember. Even though it's important to hit your targets, if you lose sight of people along the way, nothing you accomplish will have lasting significance."

Jerry took his boss's advice to heart, choosing the healthier motive from which to operate as a leader. At first, he did all he could to build his people up. But he couldn't shake a nagging fear that he might be incapable of doing his own job. He feared not only making a mistake himself, but worried that mistakes made by others on his team would reflect poorly on him.

This shifting in motives surfaced when one of Jerry's team members, Lilly, had an opportunity to conduct a series of radio interviews with high-profile authors and speakers. It would have been a boost to her career, providing her a tremendous growth opportunity, and was most likely within her capabilities. Remembering his motive to build people up, Jerry talked to Lilly about the opportunity and offered to coach her on interviewing skills in the upcoming months. But as often happens, competing priorities got in the way, urgencies came and went, and as time drew closer, Jerry realized he hadn't set aside the time he estimated was necessary to coach Lilly.

Jerry's insecurity (you might call it an unhealthy motive) kicked in. *This is a very important project. What if she blows it? What will people think of her? What will people think of me?* What he knew, but chose not to take into account, was that Lilly had been practicing on her own, and was getting prepared and excited to conduct the interviews. By most people's standards, Lilly was ready for the job. But at the last minute, Jerry defaulted to his insecurity. He lost sight of his original motive and gave the opportunity to someone he thought was more seasoned and ready for the task. Jerry resorted to autopilot without really thinking about it, and the relationship took a hit.

"Without giving her the needed coaching I'd committed to, it was too risky to let her do it," he confided in me. But I could tell the decision was bothering him.

"What motivated you to make the change?" I asked. Jerry thought it over for a moment.

"Well, I like to give people opportunities to stretch and prove themselves," he replied, "but this just wasn't the right time."

"Oh?" I asked. "And what would have made it the right time?"

Jerry started to speak, but faltered. "I don't know . . ."

Since we were friends and I knew him well, I asked, "Is it possible your *real* motive wasn't about finding an opportunity for your team member?"

"What do you mean?"

"I guess what I'm saying is that, if you had to step back and really pinpoint what was driving your decision, what would it be?"

Jerry thought it over. "Honestly, I didn't want the interview to fail. I was worried if it did, *I'd* be the one who'd have to answer for it. I'm working too hard right now to let someone else mess things up. I guess that sounds kind of harsh, but it's the truth."

We spent more time talking, and Jerry looked back at the advice his boss had given him. In a moment of personal reflection, he realized he'd lost sight of that important and healthy motive and had replaced it with an unhealthy motive driven by insecurity. His goal to invest in building others up was left unattended, and he began to slip off course—not on purpose, and not all at once, but by small degrees over time. This shift wasn't an intentional, sinister change. My friend hadn't suddenly donned a black hat, monocle, and waxed mustache (no offense meant if that's your attire of choice). That's the problem with allowing our motives to go on autopilot—it ultimately reflects the unconscious habits and routines we get sucked into, despite our good intentions (which may be why the road to hell is paved with the same).

To his credit, Jerry later apologized to Lilly and made a renewed effort to turn off his autopilot and instead examine what mattered most and make his desired, healthy motive his *real* motive.

To get to a definition of healthy versus unhealthy motives, I'd like to borrow from Dr. Martin Luther King Jr., who borrowed from St. Thomas Aquinas, when King wrote his famous letter from Birmingham City Jail, "Any law that uplifts human personality is just. Any law that degrades human personality is unjust." I think there's truth in that, and it can shed light on a new definition of motives for our purposes in this section.

Healthy motive: any motive that uplifts the human condition in ourselves and others.

Unhealthy motive: any motive that degrades the human condition in ourselves and others.

Consider the difference between an unhealthy motive—to one-up it—versus a healthy motive—to "one-plus" it. Walt Disney was highly motivated by quality, constantly challenging his artists and Imagineers to consider what was possible, then take it further. He saw each person on a team as being able to contribute, to add value, and to deliver more than what Disney's customers paid for or expected to receive: to one-plus it. Contrast that with a team where each person is vying to highlight his or her own contributions; no matter what one person accomplishes, there's a need to highlight your own achievements—to make sure you end up on top. We've all been around people who feel the need to one-up each other in a scramble to be king of the hill for a project or an accomplishment.

If we're not careful, our motives can end up being unhealthy: driven by fear, anger, or sadness in one moment and, in the next, by an unfulfilled need for acceptance, power, or safety. Too often we go on autopilot, allowing our motives to flow out of our daily routines without checking our underlying assumptions or questioning our choices. But if we examine our motives on a regular basis, we can begin to understand the difference between a motive driven by insecurity or other unmet needs, and a motive that aligns with our deepest values and develops the type of character that contributes to effective relationships.

Do you ever have an unhealthy motive? Consider the following:

- Why do you make specific comments in meetings? Do you want to add value to the discussion, or do you just want the boss to think you're smart?

- Why do you insist on doing everything yourself rather than delegating to people who are willing and able to help? Do you want to save time, or do you fear losing control?

- Why do you give unsolicited advice to your co-worker, offending him or her in the process? Is it to truly help, or do you need to feel like you are smarter than he or she is?

- Why do you never say no and often find yourself doing others' work? Do you sincerely want to provide that service, or have you convinced yourself that is the only value you add?

To help you examine your real motives, try these three things:

1. Use the 5 Whys.
2. Choose abundance.
3. Declare your intent.

USE THE 5 WHYS

The 5 Whys came to light in the late 1980s as part of the Toyota Production System for building great automobiles. Part of the system included a just-in-time technique: the 5 Whys. The approach was simple: ask "why" five times to get to the root cause of a problem. In the words of the system's pioneer, Taiichi Ohno, "Observe the production floor without preconceptions. . . . Ask 'why' five times about every matter."[9]

In borrowing this technique for human relationships, we use it to get to our root intentions or our driving motives in any situation. While it can take less (or more) than five introspective "whys" to get to our motives, because those motives may be buried under years of habit and have been running on autopilot, it often takes asking why more than once. At first, the answers to the 5 Whys might feel obvious. But if you approach the exercise honestly and with humility, thinking through it will help you understand your true motive.

Here's an example as to how the 5 Whys work. A few years ago, we were restructuring one of our divisions. We met with the division leader, John, to share the reason for the changes, the timing, and who would be affected. John was and is a great person, and although he had some strong concerns and opinions, he said he understood the decision and was supportive. John was to inform his entire team about the decision and work with HR to help those few who, as a result of the restructure, would be transitioned out of the company. We had a two-month window in which to complete the transition.

A few weeks after the initial meeting, I called John to see how it was going, and was surprised to learn he had not yet had *any* of the conversations.

"John, we now only have six weeks left," I said. "Is there any reason you are waiting?"

John told me he was wondering if we could meet again on the decision. I asked if he was no longer supportive of the decision, to which he replied, "No, I'm still supportive, but I wonder if we've considered all the ramifications."

"What other ramifications do you think we need to discuss?" I asked.

"I'm not sure," he replied.

"The longer we wait to address it, the less time those who are affected will have to start networking and looking for other opportunities," I explained.

John agreed and said he would begin making the calls the next day. Knowing John as I do, I could probably have guessed why it had taken him so long. If John had applied the 5 Whys to his procrastination, it might have sounded something like this:

1. Why am I procrastinating on making these calls? *Because I don't know if I agree with the decision.*

2. Why don't I know if I agree with the decision? *Because it's a change from how we've been operating.*

3. Why am I concerned about a change? *Because change can be difficult.*

4. Why do I believe this change will be difficult? *Because it involves asking people to do something different and difficult— something they may disagree with.*

5. Why am I worried about asking people to do something difficult that they may disagree with? *Because throughout my entire career, I've tried to avoid conflict and have struggled with conversations that involve sensitive issues.*

   My reason and real motive for procrastination in making the calls isn't because I don't agree with the decision. It's because I want to avoid conflict.

Once John and I discussed his real reason behind his delay in having the difficult conversations, I offered to join him on each of the calls. He was relieved, and we got the calls taken care of the following day.

It takes a lot of courage, humility, and self-awareness to look at ourselves closely and with honesty. If you don't see the value of examining your motives and developing your character, your motives may end up serving your ego instead of serving others. And when this shift happens, you actually perpetuate the feelings of fear, insecurity, and unmet needs of Sartre's hell.

This section isn't intended to make you feel guilty about your motives or to shame you for attempting to fill your unmet needs. It is, however, intended to help you become more aware of any unhealthy motives so that you can choose to redirect them toward healthier, more abundant motives. When you recognize that your motives are driven by something other than to *uplift the human condition* in yourself and others, be patient with the part of you that's trying to get what it needs. However, also recognize that another part of you can choose a different motive. Once we identify an unhealthy motive, how do we move to a healthier one? Try choosing abundance.

CHOOSE ABUNDANCE

Many of us are conditioned to believe that there's a finite amount of everything—that there's only so much reward, credit, recognition, benefits, or even love. And because of that, the more *you* get means there's less for *me*. This belief creates what we at FranklinCovey call a scarcity mindset, which produces an underlying motive of fear. With a fearful world view, it's difficult to shift the focus off ourselves and take the needs of others into consideration.

One of my key takeaways from the book *Discover Your Sales Strengths*, by Benson Smith and Tony Rutigliano, is that the best salespeople don't always make the best sales leaders. Why? Because top revenue producers are often competitive—which salespeople should be. When an independent salesperson is asked to lead a group of people who may end up making more money than he or she does, for some it may be difficult to think interdependently—to redefine success and switch the motivation from personal gain to collective success. Unless they can dig deeper to care as much about the group winning as they care about themselves winning, they'll struggle to create a working environment optimized for team performance.

By contrast, I remember a recent example of a seasoned executive who showcased what an abundance mindset looks like. He worked in the hospitality industry, and had invited our CEO and executive team to meet and participate in a weekly meeting. Having recently implemented some of our content and processes, the hotel leaders wanted to showcase their newly acquired business-execution capabilities.

The property general manager welcomed us to the meeting and

informed us the hotel was one of their flagship properties employing
nearly four thousand people. He admitted that with such a large staff,
some days it felt like he was running a city more than a hotel. Prior
to inviting the divisional leaders in to present their results, the general
manager spent some time with us describing their culture, including
the successes they'd achieved and some of the challenges they were
still facing. He informed us that he'd invited leaders from all the major
operations to join the weekly meeting: housekeeping, food and bever-
age, engineering, sales and catering, and more. Before they came in,
he let us know that he wanted to share his personal vision for each of
them with us.

"As an employee of this organization for twenty-plus years, and
a veteran of the industry for many more," he reported broadly yet
humbly, "I've experienced a phenomenal journey. As such, I've been
privileged to earn our company's President's Club Award with its accompanying incentive trip numerous times, and I've cherished the experience over many years."

He then went on to say something I'll never forget: "But now that
I have all the glass and crystal trophies one could ever want or need
in a lifetime, I want my goal to be clear. Actually, not my goal; what
I am talking about is my legacy. I want to ensure that each person on
my team—each person about to walk into this room and report—earn
their accolades. I want each of them to achieve the President's Club and
more. And as they do, I want them to pass that same vision on to their
associates, and so on, over the many years that follow."

You could see and truly feel that this man's intent was pure. He
cast a vision broader than his own success to the larger successes of his
team. I suspected that such a view was a key contribution to why he
had risen to such heights within the organization in the first place.

To examine whether you come from a scarcity or an abundance
mindset, read each phrase below and circle where you think you are
on the continuum:

There is only so much and the more
you get, the less there is for me.

There is plenty out
there for everyone.

| 1 | 2 | 3 | 4 | 5 | 6 | 7 | 8 | 9 | 10 |

I'm threatened by the success of others,
especially those closest to me.

I'm happy for the
success of others.

| 1 | 2 | 3 | 4 | 5 | 6 | 7 | 8 | 9 | 10 |

I treat people with varying degrees of
respect based on position or status.

I treat *everyone*
with equal respect.

| 1 | 2 | 3 | 4 | 5 | 6 | 7 | 8 | 9 | 10 |

I have a difficult time sharing
recognition or credit.

I find it easy to share
recognition or credit.

| 1 | 2 | 3 | 4 | 5 | 6 | 7 | 8 | 9 | 10 |

I find my sense of self-worth from being
compared to others or from competition.

I have a deep inner sense
of self-worth and security.

| 1 | 2 | 3 | 4 | 5 | 6 | 7 | 8 | 9 | 10 |

If you scored low in any area, practice thinking abundantly. Instead of dwelling on what you don't have, begin to focus on what you do have. Take time to appreciate or express gratitude for what is there, rather than complain about what isn't. Look for ways to share your abundance with others.

An abundance mindset is the primary foundation for establishing ongoing healthy motives. As you build this authentic, sincere, and positive outlook, it will be a key contributor in influencing for good the people around you.

DECLARE INTENT

Stephen M. R. Covey is Dr. Covey's eldest son, CEO of the former Covey Leadership Center, and author of the bestselling book *The Speed of Trust*. Stephen M. R. writes, "Declare your intent. Express your agenda and motives. Then be true to your intent."[10] Intent is another word for motives. Declaring your motives is one of the core behaviors that builds trust.

While we judge ourselves largely on our intentions, others judge us by our behavior. Have you ever been driving when someone in the lane next to you, without warning, decides to change lanes? Every time it happens to me, I'm alarmed and somewhat angry. While I don't think most people want to intentionally scare or harm me, I do think they're careless. They forget to use their turn signal, and don't think about the potential negative impact of their uncommunicated intention. The same thing happens when we fail to share our intentions or motives with others, especially when beginning a difficult conversation, starting a meeting, or writing an important email. As I mentioned in the beginning of the practice, only you know your real motive. However, sometimes if we don't communicate it early on, we end up putting others in the position of assuming or guessing, like the person changing lanes without signaling. You can easily put others at ease (and avoid a lot of misunderstanding) when you declare your intent as often and as soon as you can.

Not too long ago, I had a difficult conversation with one of my associates, Drew. Because of a decline in performance, we put him on a written performance plan—a step we take to give an employee an opportunity to meet his or her established goals and objectives. At the beginning of the meeting with him and his boss, I said, "Drew, I want you to know that our only intent in this discussion and this performance plan is to help you be successful in your role. We want to share with you where we see gaps in your performance so we can help you improve in those areas. That is our only intent."

It was a tough conversation. Yet, because Drew knew we were trying to help him and not simply get rid of him, we were able to be transparent. Months later, Drew approached me; he'd been doing great while working through his performance plan.

"Todd," he confessed, "I want you to know how nervous and uncomfortable I was in that first meeting. I was so nervous that I couldn't hear anything anyone was saying. But when you told me your 'only intent' was to help me succeed, my fear subsided. I believed you. So I could start to listen and hear what was being said."

You don't need to wait for an extreme situation like Drew's to declare your intentions. There is no downside in sharing your intentions (unless you have bad intentions, in which case you may want to read my sequel titled *Get Worse: 15 Practices to Destroy Relationships, Lose Trust, and Be Unfriended on Social Media*).

On another occasion, our IT department came to me with a serious problem—one of our employees (I'll call him Taylor) was spending time at work visiting inappropriate websites on his company computer. It was my job to confront him and have what can only be described as a very awkward conversation. After considering how to handle the topic, I invited him to my office. I could have started with our policy handbook and read the section dealing with appropriate use of company assets, or I could have cited the report from the IT department that connected the IP address of his computer to various websites. Instead, I decided to start by declaring my intent. I thanked him for meeting with me and said, "Taylor, I need to talk with you about something very serious. I have a lot of respect for you, and what we need to discuss is important enough that, if you don't get it corrected, you're at risk of losing your job. Please know that my intent is to make sure that doesn't happen."

We then went on to discuss the situation. Taylor could have denied it, made excuses, or even blamed someone else. But he didn't. He owned it and assured me it would never happen again.

Sometime later, after he'd transferred out of state, we ran into each other at an airport and briefly got caught up. As we finished and I turned to walk toward my gate, he said, "Hey, Todd, can I share something with you? I know I put you in a very awkward situation several years ago. I just wanted to say how much I appreciated the way you dealt with it. I don't know if you remember, but you told me that your intent was to help me keep my job. You could have handled the conversation quite differently. Even though I didn't feel I deserved it, you treated me with respect."

Declaring intent serves several purposes:

- It provides a safe environment for a relationship to thrive, allowing the other person to respond to what's really going on rather than having to guess and get suspicious of what's happening below the surface.

- It creates transparency and stability. If left unspoken, your motive is more likely to shift when high emotion is present or when a circumstance might tempt you to change directions.

- It can anchor everyone involved in the motive so that people are operating on the same page. It lets people know what to look for, recognize, understand, and acknowledge.

While there's little downside to declaring your intent, it's especially important when emotions are high or when you don't know the Emotional Bank Account balance in the relationship. (See "Practice 8: Take Stock of Your Emotional Bank Accounts" for more on this topic.)

Without stopping to examine the motives that have largely gone on autopilot and have been buried under the routines and unconscious habits of our daily lives, we can't become intentional about transforming them into healthy ones, something Sam was about to experience firsthand over his breakfast meeting with Kevin.

● ● ●

Kevin sent an email to Sam, requesting a breakfast meeting for the next morning, which Sam accepted. "Maybe I'll tell him I quit," he thought to himself. "At the very least, I'm going to let him know I'm tired of him taking credit for everyone's work. What is he thinking?"

The next morning they met at a nearby restaurant. Sam reached out and shook Kevin's hand but immediately sensed something was wrong. After they took their seats, Kevin opened up.

"I'm kind of surprised by your email to the company," Kevin said. "You know how much work I put into the proposal—how many nights and weekends I labored over it. But you didn't mention any of that. It sounded like the whole technology strategy was your idea."

The accusation hit Sam with a force that almost felt physical. "I always give you credit, Kevin."

Kevin responded, "Sure, you give me credit when we're talking one-on-one. But it feels like when it comes to things like company email announcements, because it comes from you, it sounds like you're doing all the work."

A number of thoughts ran through Sam's mind. "Could he be right? Do I really not give my team credit when in public? Why would I do that?"

"Is there a reason you didn't mention I was the one who put the plan together?" Kevin asked.

"No, I don't think so," Sam said. He apologized and told Kevin he'd given him a lot to think about.

While Sam hadn't been actively working to take credit for other people's efforts, deep inside, an unconscious motive was running on autopilot, one that yearned to make sure everyone in the company saw him as an innovative and a successful leader—a motive that was operating at the expense of the people he was attempting to lead.

In the following days and weeks, Sam thought about what Kevin had said: "Why am I not giving more credit to members of the team?"

"Because it makes you look good," a silent voice answered in the back of his mind.

It was a watershed moment for Sam. He later met with Kevin and asked, "Do you think you could give me a chance to correct my mistake?"

"Of course," Kevin said.

"From now on," Sam responded, *"you have my commitment to publicly recognize you and the team in the future, including involving them in the communications that go out to the company."*

As I've worked with Sam over the years, I've seen him stop and examine his motives as we've discussed his various projects and the personalities of those he works with. There's power in understanding our motives and being intentional about them as we work to develop our relationships with others.

EXAMINE YOUR REAL MOTIVES

Be your own forensic examiner.

1. Identify a high-stakes situation and clearly describe the outcome you want.

2. Ask yourself "why?" as many times as necessary to identify your underlying reasons for wanting the outcome. (Be as honest as you can about your motives.)

   1. Why? _____

   2. Why? _____

   3. Why? _____

   4. Why? _____

   5. Why? _____

3. After listing the motives, ask yourself these questions:

   a. Which motives are self-serving and need my attention (unhealthy)? Mark them with an "x."

   b. Which motives serve the whole—myself and others (healthy)? Mark them with a circle.

   c. Which motives are most aligned with my values? Mark them with a star.

4. If others were to observe you acting on any self-serving motives (marked with an "x"), what would they see and how would they feel? Write your answer below.

5. If others were to observe you acting on the motives most aligned with your values (marked with a star), what would they see and how would they feel? Write your answer below.

6. Choose which motives you will act on going forward.

TALK LESS, LISTEN MORE

DO YOU LISTEN TO OTHERS WITH THE INTENT TO REPLY OR TO UNDERSTAND?

If you listen with the intent to reply, you may want to consider

PRACTICE 10: TALK LESS, LISTEN MORE.

When you don't talk less and listen more, your room may feel like Sartre's hell because:

- You rarely get to the heart of an issue, if at all.
- You lose the opportunity to be influenced by others and, in turn, have greater influence yourself.
- You alienate people who might otherwise respect and confide in you.

*Imagine one of those 1950s sitcoms on a black-and-white TV set where,
after the appropriately cheesy opening-theme music, we find a married
couple about to have two very different conversations at the same time. It
might go something like this:*

John sits at the kitchen table, his trusty old vacuum cleaner in pieces as
he flips through the ragged pages of the owner's manual. He hardly notices
Barbara, his wife, who takes a seat opposite him.

"John, I need to talk to you. It's important."

"Sure, sure," John replies as he picks up a screwdriver and begins fiddling with something.

Barbara frowns. "Are you listening to me?"

"Of course I am, dear," John answers as pleasantly as he can, turning
the screw and releasing the old vacuum's dust bag.

His wife takes a breath. "I think we should invite my mother to move
in with us," she exclaims, looking at John nervously.

John shakes his head, frowning at the broken-down vacuum on the
table in front of him. "There's something wrong with the old bag if you ask
me."

"John!" his wife exclaims. "That's my mother you're referring to!"

John grunts absentmindedly as he turns a part over. "Definitely got a
screw or two loose."

Barbara gasps and folds her arms. "I never knew you had such animosity in you!"

John sighs, the vacuum cleaner getting the best of him. "You know,
there's just a point when the old girl is so broken down it's not worth trying
to keep her around anymore. Just takes up space, never works when you
need her to, and honestly, ever since last summer, she kind of smells funny."

"Well, I never!" Barbara exclaims, standing and storming off. John
looks up from his project, more confused than ever. "I'm sorry, did you say
something, dear?"

The television audience breaks out in laughter as the episode breaks for
a commercial.

● ● ●

Television writers have used miscommunication to great effect over the years. Unfortunately, when it comes to real-life relationships, our propensity to talk more than we listen can get us into real trouble. Of course, in the rush to solve problems and get things done, there's a natural tendency for all of us to simply *tell*. And we're quite good at it. Think of the great communication classes you may have had over the years. While called "communication," they were all about how to *deliver* or *present* a message. I challenge you to find one that was about how to effectively *listen*.

Of the various aphorisms handed down by the ancient Greeks, perhaps Zeno of Citium offered one of the most practical: "We have two ears and one mouth, so we should listen more than we say." Now, you can't argue with logic like that. And the truth is, when we take it upon ourselves to do all the talking, we almost always pay a price.

Making quick decisions and judgment calls will often lead to misdiagnosed solutions, faulty assumptions, narrow perspectives, and misunderstood facts. As a result, we deprive others of the opportunity to solve problems on their own. If losing out on the efficacy of our plans weren't a steep enough price to pay, when we fail to take time to truly listen, we threaten trust. Imagine having a sore throat and headache and going to a doctor, but instead of her listening to you describe your symptoms, she takes one look at your knees and writes a prescription for physical therapy. Would you ever return for another visit? Would you trust the doctor again? While this example may sound ludicrous, many of us prescribe before we diagnose all the time.

I got my first taste of the downside of not listening as a youth when my father was the coach of our Little League baseball team. I wasn't a natural athlete, and playing baseball wasn't my number-one priority. Despite all the time with my dad, our practices, and even our games, I rarely paid attention to instructions about the game, and instead used the time as my social hour to catch up with friends. After several games in which I struck out repeatedly, I was next up to bat during a particularly close game. I routinely dreaded this position, as I could vividly picture myself swinging and striking out yet again. However, as I watched the batter ahead of me, I noticed that he wasn't swinging at the ball at all. And then, incredibly, after four successive pitches and four refusals to swing, the umpire waved him on. I watched in astonishment as he slowly jogged to first base, without a care in the world. This new information changed everything! I'd finally figured out how to save face and get around the bases at the same time.

I eagerly took my spot over home plate with a whole new appreciation for the sport. I loved the idea of not swinging at the ball, then walking to first base. Why hadn't anyone let me in on this liberating option? So I did just that. I rested the bat on my shoulder and not even once thought about taking a swing. I vaguely remember my dad and the other players yelling at me. But again, I wasn't listening; it was just noise. I knew what I wanted to do, and I was determined to do it.

Three pitches came in successive order. Then, to my surprise, the umpire yelled, "Strike three, you're out!"

"What?" I said, not understanding what was going on.

As I moped my way back, passing the next batter on my way to the dugout, I wondered, *What did I do wrong? Didn't I not swing just like I was supposed to? If Greg got to walk to first base without swinging, why do I have to go back to the dugout?*

After a long and uncomfortable drive home with Coach Dad, I realized that talking to friends during practices instead of listening to learn the difference between a ball and a strike had failed me. Even up at bat, when I had a final chance to understand, I was so focused on what I wanted (an easy walk to first base) that I didn't hear all the good advice being yelled at me, and I misinterpreted the events that unfolded. Although embarrassing at the time, it was a good lesson to learn: one of the best ways to avoid looking like a fool is to listen to the people around you, especially your dad.

THE DOWNSIDE OF TALKING MORE AND LISTENING LESS

Think about a time when you felt misunderstood by someone. How did it make you feel? Maybe you got defensive and vented your anger and frustration. Or maybe you felt intimidated or shut down, perhaps committing never to open up to that person again. Regardless of the response, each time we feel misunderstood (not truly heard) by someone important to us, we can feel disrespected and hurt. We may even experience an unintentional breach of trust, as if an essential part of the relationship bond had been chipped away.

I remember working at a previous company with Gary, a new salesperson, who worked diligently to try to acquire a potential client's business. Getting the account would be the largest deal he'd created to date and would have allowed him to reach his yearly revenue goal— which would qualify him for a nice bonus and a spot in the coveted President's Club. Over a seven-month period, Gary met with the potential client several times, discovering what he thought were their major concerns. He then tried (perhaps a little too hard) to frame the conversations in a way that favored the solutions he had for solving their specific issues. He was confident he had what they needed.

Just when Gary thought the client was ready to seal the deal and sign a contract, he got a call from them. "Thank you so much for the time you spent consulting with us. But after talking with my partners, we've decided to go in a different direction." Gary was devastated. After getting over the initial disappointment, he was curious to understand what was behind the client's decision and called his contact a few days later.

"We've found a different vendor that better addresses a unique problem we're facing," the man told Gary, sharing more of the problem and why it had been so troubling to them.

Gary was perplexed as he listened to the explanation. "But we never even discussed that in all of the conversations we had together," he replied.

"Exactly," the man continued. "To be honest, I tried to explain our challenges in a couple of meetings, but the conversation kept changing to the solution you had and how perfect it was for our needs. And frankly, the questions the other vendor asked helped us uncover an underlying issue that we didn't think mattered at first. Once she helped us uncover it, we knew her solution would fit better and that she understood our needs."

Gary learned a difficult but valuable lesson that day. By being too quick to offer a solution, he missed the opportunity to listen and uncover the real issue needing to be solved.

"WISDOM IS THE REWARD YOU GET FOR A LIFETIME OF LISTENING WHEN YOU'D HAVE PREFERRED TO TALK."

—DOUG LARSON, NEWSPAPER COLUMNIST

THE UPSIDE OF TALKING LESS AND LISTENING MORE

One of the most profound gifts you can give another human being is your sincere understanding. To do so requires clearing away your mental clutter, suspending (at least temporarily) your agenda, and stopping long enough to focus and hear what someone is really saying. When it comes to creating effective relationships, a famous adage I'm often mindful of is: *With people, fast is slow and slow is fast.* An attentive, unbiased, listening ear gives people the rare opportunity to feel understood—a gift some psychologists argue we need as much as the air we breathe. (I assume most of those psychologists are not deep-sea divers, but it's still a good point.) Being truly present provides a safe environment in which people can learn to listen to themselves, assess their own behavior, diagnose their own problems, and come up with their own solutions.

I can't tell you how many times when people come to me to solve a problem, they end up solving it themselves. By the end of the conversation (which really amounts to my simply talking less and listening more), they know what they need to do. For instance, last week an employee, Alec, came to me complaining about what he believed was an unfair workload distribution on a team project.

"This happens to me all the time," he said with some anger. "Remember last year when I ended up taking on twice the number of assignments as everyone else?"

"It seems like you're feeling that you frequently get the short end of the stick," I replied. And for the next hour, that's about all I said. I sat there listening, occasionally paraphrasing back to him what he'd said. Here are some of the phrases I used during the conversation:

"Sounds like you're feeling overwhelmed."

"You don't feel that others are carrying the same burden as you?"

"It seems like balancing work and your personal life is becoming more of a challenge."

I also asked a few clarifying questions along the way:

"Remind me what happened last year and how you handled the additional work at that time."

"I know your team leader relies on you a lot. Does he know how you feel?"

The more Alec talked and the more I listened, the more he understood what *he* needed to do. With space to explore his own thoughts and feelings, he came up with an idea. We ended the meeting with Alec rehearsing a very brave yet considerate conversation he was going to have with his boss.

"Thanks for talking. You always have great advice," he said as he left. I smiled after he walked out. I hadn't advised him at all! He ended up advising himself. In this case, that was the key.

REASONS WE DON'T TALK LESS AND LISTEN MORE

Besides our crazy, busy lives, what else causes us to talk more and listen less? Let me offer a few ideas:

1. **We're trained to talk more.** As was stated earlier, we take all sorts of classes to become better communicators, speakers, or more persuasive negotiators. But we rarely take classes on how to listen.

2. **We're fixers by nature.** Most of us want to jump to a solution as soon as possible. And not with malicious intent; we just want to help. We tend to acknowledge the fixers as those worthy of praise.

3. **The world is in a hurry.** In today's world, we live in a sound-bite society. Information is coming at us twenty-four/ seven. All of our communication styles have devolved into "How fast can we communicate?" And it's become almost commonplace to see how fast we can interrupt each other.

4. **We want to be right.** Dr. Covey summed it up this way: "If you're like most people, you want to seek first to be understood; you want to get your point across. And in doing so, you may ignore the other person completely, pretend that you're listening, selectively hear only certain parts of the conversation, or attentively focus on only the words being said, but miss the meaning entirely. Most people listen with the intent to reply, not to understand."

Many of these reasons can be summed up in what we at Franklin-Covey call *autobiographical listening*. Simply put, everything you think and say comes from your point of view. You listen to yourself (your own story) while others are talking, preparing in your mind what you want to say or what you want to ask. You filter everything you hear through your own experiences. And then you check what you hear against your own story to see how it compares. When you engage in autobiographical listening, you end up deciding prematurely what people mean before they finish talking, which can create huge communication divides.

Autobiographical listening can lead to giving people advice before they've asked for it:

"Oh, I had that same problem a few years ago, and what I did was . . ."

"I think you're ignoring the facts."

"When I had your job, I just told them to . . ."

"If I were you, I would prepare the meeting this way . . ."

Autobiographical listening can lead to asking too many questions—not to get more understanding on an issue, but to satisfy our own curiosity:

"So where were you when this happened?"

"Why did you say that?"

"What were you trying to accomplish by using that approach?"

Unfortunately, when we filter what others say through our own stories and experiences, we draw conclusions based on what *we* might do or feel in the same situation. Or worse, because we might be uncomfortable with the situation, we prescribe a solution that makes *us* feel better. We're often afraid that if we listen too closely, we may be influenced and not get our way. While it's natural to do so, jumping to conclusions or replying too soon with advice can make people feel like we are judging or evaluating them—certainly not listening to them. It can also make people dig in their heels even more, investing in their own point of view and being less open to looking at other alternatives.

• • •

Corinne had grown up in the United Kingdom, but worked in the United States for a decade and a half. While she missed her family, she had made a life in the States and was amazingly adept at leading high-profile projects for her company. During one of those projects, she got an emergency call from a hospital in Manchester, letting her know that her father had died suddenly and unexpectedly. It hit her hard—she hadn't had time to prepare nor had she been there for him and her family. A few short weeks later, after Corinne had returned from his funeral, her mother had a series of illnesses resulting in two hip replacements and a heart attack. Afraid of losing her mom so soon, and not wanting to be so far away from her during an important time, Corinne took four trips to Manchester in a little over fourteen months to help care for her mother. When she returned to work after each visit, she reported that her mother was getting increasingly depressed and weary of trying to recuperate from all of the loss.

Understandably, her mom started losing the will to improve, avoiding physical-therapy appointments and isolating herself. Barely home after the fourth trip, exhausted emotionally and physically herself, Corinne got a call from her mom's doctor who relayed the latest news: Her mother was badly in need of triple bypass heart surgery. If she didn't make a concerted, genuine effort to recuperate from her previous hip surgeries, her mother would most certainly be dead in less than a year. The problem was, her mother was opposed to another surgery.

"I'm not going to do this, Corinne. I'm not up for it, and I can't manage it," her mother told her over the phone. Fearful of losing her mother, and on the heels of spending a great deal of effort to help her recuperate, Corinne began slipping into an autobiographical response: *You have to have this surgery! You can't give up. You have to go forward with it.*

Instead, Corinne stopped herself, letting go of her wants and fears. Rather than arguing with her mother, and either manipulating her or telling her what to do, she simply listened. As her mother shared her fears, Corinne began to see things through her mother's eyes. "It sounds like you're really concerned about going into the hospital again," she replied. And later, "I really get it when you say the past eighteen months have been so difficult, and that you don't think you can manage this on your own."

Corinne spent about thirty minutes really listening, not with the intent of getting her mom to switch to Corinne's agenda, but simply trying to understand and empathize. Finally, after going back and forth expressing fear and anxiety, her mother said, "You know, I really want to be here when the grandkids grow up."

Even then, instead of jumping on that encouraging phrase to turn the conversation toward her own agenda, Corinne simply reflected back what her mom had said and felt: "That's pretty special, isn't it, being able to be part of their lives?"

"Yes, I want to see more of my grandkids. It's become even more important to me to spend time with them as I've become older." Corinne's mother opened up, finally asking, "Do you think you could come home one more time when I have the surgery?"

"Yes, Mom, I can do that."

There was a moment of silence before Corinne's mom continued. "Okay, I'll do it."

During the entire conversation, Corinne never suggested her mom have surgery, even though that's what she desperately wanted. By listening just to understand, she was able to suspend her agenda, allowing her to hear how painful her mother's previous surgeries had been, and how alone and afraid she'd become. Corinne realized that it wasn't fair to foist her own anxiety on her mom—that her mother had a right to make decisions for her own life. By the end of the call, Corinne was feeling so much empathy for her ailing parent, that if her mom had decided not to go through with the procedure, Corinne would have supported the decision.

Two months later, Corinne flew to the United Kingdom, and was there for her mother's recovery. She later told me she wasn't sure if her mom would even still be here if she hadn't taken time to really hear her on the phone that day.

HOW TO TALK LESS AND LISTEN MORE

It's important to note that while there are several skills to listening well, none of them are as important as having the right attitude while listening. If you're good at the skill but aren't sincerely interested in understanding the other person, you'll fail. In contrast, if you don't get the skill right, but your intentions are sincere, people will feel your genuine concern and often give you the benefit of a doubt.

Before we get into the specifics, please understand that talking less and listening more is not the same as agreeing with people. When I talk about listening, people often push back: "I can't let them go on and on. I don't want them thinking I agree with them." You may ultimately disagree with what a person is saying or feeling, but while you're listening, you're not imposing your views on the person. You're not trying to figure out how to get him or her to see it your way. In- stead, you're suspending your opinions long enough to really step into that individual's world and try to understand it from his or her point of view. This approach sounds simple, but it's one of the most difficult mindsets to master, especially if you're diametrically opposed to that person's point of view or emotionally involved. It takes an incredibly mature person to master this skill. (See all other practices in this book for details on how to increase your maturity level.)

A few years ago we made a change in the pay plan for our sales leaders. One of our highest-producing individuals emailed me and communicated just how upset he was about the change. My phone rang, and I saw his name pop up.

"Thanks for taking my call, Todd," he said.

"You're welcome. I know you have a lot of questions about why we made the change, which I'm happy to answer. But first, I really want to hear your concerns. So I'm just going to listen."

"I want to give you context for why I'm upset and share with you how a few of my colleagues are feeling," he continued.

"Okay," I responded. "That would be helpful." He spent the rest of the call sharing his frustrations and the impact the new plan was having on his and others' compensation. Several times I reflected back what I heard him saying—not agreeing or disagreeing with him; just seeking to understand. Here are a few things you might have overheard during the call:

> "You don't feel that your compensation should be tied so closely to a new salesperson's revenue who reports to you?"

> "You sound pretty frustrated with the new plan."

> "You feel like our pay plans have changed too frequently?"

I also asked several clarifying questions during the call:

> "What would you have done differently in communicating the sales plan?"

> "What revenue goal do you believe is possible to achieve with your new people?"

> "What could we do in supporting you to achieve that goal?"

Once he felt comfortable that my intent was to understand, he started to ask more questions about why we'd switched plans. I explained the reasons as best I could. We were into the conversation about thirty minutes when, to my surprise, he said, "I wish we could have waited until the end of the year to make this change. But after talking, I don't know if there will be a better time than now. You know, I'd probably do the same thing if I were in charge." Because I didn't jump in to explain or defend the corporate position, my colleague had a chance to vent. Once he felt understood, he was in a better position to return the favor and listen to another point of view.

Now, please don't misunderstand—I'm not saying that all you have to do is listen and solutions will magically appear. There are appropriate times to talk *more* and listen *less*. Often it's necessary to give advice and provide clear answers and direction to get the job done. But there are times when it's also vital to do the opposite. When a person is highly emotional, or when the Emotional Bank Account balance is low (see "Practice 8: Take Stock of Your Emotional Bank Accounts"), or you're not sure you fully understand, you'll almost always benefit from talking less. By carefully listening and understanding first, before you advise or give solutions, you are in a much better position to grasp the real issues. Once you accurately address the situation as well as the person's feelings, he or she will feel more respected and trust will grow.

Once you have the attitude of really listening, it's time to apply the skill. It's counterintuitive yet ridiculously simple. Essentially, it's the ability to reflect back to people what they are saying and what they are feeling. But when it's done earnestly and authentically, it creates magic: it brings the speaker to a greater awareness of what he or she is feeling; it brings the listener into a rare state of empathy, and it creates a trust and rapport in the relationship that can't be matched.

THE IMPACT OF TALKING LESS, LISTENING MORE

Years ago in one or our training courses, we had a very powerful activity where we would test how close individuals could come to understanding another's point of view, and how open they would be to the accompanying vulnerability. We did this by sharing the following true story:

• • •

At the age of nineteen, DB Richards (fictitious name) was drafted into the Vietnam War. After a year of combat, he was home on a leave and got into a scuffle at a local pub. The pub's owner got those involved to move outside, where the arguing continued. At one point, DB pulled out a gun and fired it, later saying he did so only to disperse the crowd. Unfortunately, the bullet struck and killed a young man. DB was imprisoned with a ten-year sentence, but in his second year, he escaped. He climbed under a fence and disappeared into society. During the next twenty-five years, he got a job, paid taxes, and bought a home. He never had any further brushes with the law and lived by himself. Eventually, the sister of the young man who had been killed located DB on the internet and had the police arrest him.

At this point in the activity, we would ask class participants what they would do with DB if they were the judge and jury. They had to choose between lock him up or let him go. The class was almost always equally divided between the two options. Each participant was paired up with someone who had the opposing view. Then together, they would be instructed to take turns listening to each other without talking. Only when one person felt completely understood about their position could the other person then share their perspective. It was a fascinating activity to discuss afterward. Time and time again, I would hear participants share how surprised they were at the change in their line of thinking once they had taken time to understand the perspective of another. Rarely would anyone announce that they had completely changed their mind. But they would say, "I can absolutely understand why my colleague feels the way they do, and I'm starting to see this a little differently now."

Talking less and listening more feels risky. It's a practice only highly emotionally mature people can master. When we are mature and confident enough to set aside our own agenda long enough to get into the hearts and minds of those important to us, we not only get to solutions more quickly, but we offer them our best selves. The reward for talking less and listening more is a deep understanding of one another. As Dr. Covey said, "The deepest need of the human heart is to feel understood." When I first heard that quote, while it seemed to make sense, I wondered if it were true. But after years of experience with the most important people in my life, I can say, for me at least, it is true 100 percent of the time.

TALK LESS, LISTEN MORE

Start practicing talking less and listening more.

---

1. Identify an important person in your life who could benefit from being truly listened to.

2. Have a conversation with that person with the sole intent of listening to understand, not to reply.

3. During the conversation, remember you don't need to agree or disagree with them. Just paraphrase what you hear, reflecting both what they say and how they feel back to them. (Note: You can also not say anything at all, and just listen!)

4. Describe your experience and what you learned with a trusted colleague or friend.

GET YOUR VOLUME RIGHT

HAVE YOU EVER HAD ONE OF YOUR GO-TO STRENGTHS STOP WORKING FOR YOU?

If so, you may want to consider

PRACTICE 11: GET YOUR VOLUME RIGHT.

When you don't get your volume right, your room may feel like Sartre's hell because:

- You're not sure why people respond negatively to your strengths, and it shakes your confidence.
- People misinterpret your intentions because they can't see past the noise, then they start to avoid you.
- "Strengths overkill" may limit your career and credibility.

Facing the prospect of a Saturday-morning to-do list on a day far too nice to be stuck inside, I welcomed an unexpected call from an old acquaintance, Thomas. He announced he was looking for a last-minute golf partner and wondered if I could fill in. Thomas knew I wasn't much of a golfer, and I typically had as much fun driving the cart as I did actually golfing. But I assumed he was more interested in my company than my golfing prowess, which was just fine with me. I traded the to-do list for my clubs and headed out the door.

I found Thomas in the parking lot a few minutes later. He was on his phone looking flustered. "Of course, I understand the ramifications," Thomas said as he paced back and forth, "but I don't think we should release it until we're all satisfied."

Tom caught sight of me and motioned me over. "I'm not as worried about how long it takes," he continued, rubbing his temple with his free hand, "it's about it being right. And I don't mean mostly right—I mean every line of code needs to be flawless. So I think we just need to delay the launch until we're all satisfied." Thomas slipped the phone into his pocket and headed my way.

"Sorry about that," he said as we met and shook hands. "Just a little head-butting with the partners. But anyway, thanks for coming on such short notice."

"My pleasure," I replied. "Thanks for the invite. Everything okay?"

"Yeah," Thomas said. "I just think it's important we pay the price to get things right, and it's frustrating." I knew Thomas worked at a software company that did something with Web analytics, but as a guy who thought flip phones were still pretty neat, I figured whatever he was talking about was likely way over my head.

"This way," Thomas announced, motioning toward the clubhouse. We walked from the parking lot to a paved path as I looked at my watch.

"Looks like I barely made it in time."

"Oh, we're good," Thomas said, suddenly veering over to a small bench. He set his clubs down and took a seat. "Just give me a second."

"Uh, sure," I replied, watching as he produced a small towel, several small brushes, a can of foaming cleanser, and a pick tool from his bag. He removed a club, sprayed it with the foam, and then began to wipe it.

"Forget to clean that one, huh?" I asked, watching as a pair of golfers walked past.

"Keeping the face clean is essential to good performance," Thomas replied.

"You don't say . . ."

"Same reason professional caddies wipe their players' clubs after every shot." Thomas finished with the towel, but instead of retrieving the next club, he grabbed a small brush and began working on the individual grooves. *"If you have any dirt or grass in there, it will change the ball's spin. And, of course, getting a consistent spin produces better accuracy."* (The amount of time I've thought about getting a consistent spin on my golf ball is roughly the same amount of time I've thought about becoming a professional cage fighter. Which is to say, not a lot.)

"Well, we all want better accuracy," I agreed.

"It's just like coding—you have to take the time you need to get it right," Thomas said, giving the club a final look before sliding it back into his bag and reaching for another. My heart sank as I thought about the thirteen others waiting to be similarly attended to. I glanced at my watch.

"Looks like we're up now," I offered. *"If we hurry, we can probably make it."*

"Great," Thomas replied. But if he was worried about being late, he didn't show it. Instead, he repeated the foam, towel, and brush routine. *"Do you know what the average golf score was in 1960?"* he asked as he continued his work.

"Uh . . . nope."

"One hundred," Thomas replied, exchanging his now-clean club for the next one. *"Just think of everything that's happened in the last fifty years—innovations in clubs, how we teach and practice, and all the new technology. All these big changes and guess what the average score is today?"*

"No idea."

"One hundred. So that tells you something."

"It does?" I asked, glancing nervously at the clubhouse as another pair of golfers walked past.

"It tells you that it's not the big things that make a difference. It's the little things—stuff people don't think about. Like keeping your club faces clean."

"I could give you a hand if you'd like . . ." I offered.

"Thanks, but I'm kind of particular about how I do it. No offense."

"None taken," I said, putting my own clubs down and taking a seat on the bench. I had the feeling it was going to be a while.

It took nearly twenty minutes before we made it to the tee box. The teenager at the pro shop did his best to shuffle the schedule and squeeze us in. Thomas thanked him, missing the annoyed glances from the others who had showed up on time. Back outside, I pulled my driver from the bag and couldn't help but notice a pair of golfers who were waiting for us, arms crossed and glaring.

"It's worth the time it takes to do things right," Thomas announced as he prepared for his swing. "You'll see."

● ● ●

We all have natural strengths (in Thomas's case, an acute attention to detail). In defining strengths generally, the *Oxford English Dictionary* uses descriptors such as influence, power, intensity, and potency. Utilizing and nurturing our unique bundle of strengths is a fundamental part of who we are. Whether as talents we were born with or skills we developed over time, our strengths are often our go-to way for getting things done. They've become so ingrained in our behavior, we often don't think about how we're using them or the impact they're having on others.

I'd like you to imagine that using your strengths is like a musician performing on stage. For the music to have the intended effect, it requires the right volume as well as the right venue.

THE RIGHT VOLUME

Think of your strengths like the knob on an amplifier. As you turn it to a higher setting, you're rewarded with more volume. Have you ever worn headphones on a run or at the gym? Often the volume we first choose feels inadequate after a few minutes, so we inch the level up. If you're like me, this notching up of the volume can happen several times over the course of one workout. The tendency to continually raise the volume happens so regularly that many audio devices come with warnings to let you know you might be putting your hearing at risk. It seems odd, doesn't it, that we could be raising the volume to such a degree that we don't realize it's doing us harm?

It reminds me of the time I needed to borrow my son's car. When I turned the key, the stereo roared to life. It was so loud, it practically committed assault on my eardrums. I scrambled to find the button to turn it down, but since I didn't drive the car very often, it took some random and somewhat frantic button mashing before I found it. As I sat there, my ears still ringing, I wondered how in the world my son could safely and effectively drive with the volume so high.

Our strengths often function in the same way. We grow accustomed to using them at a certain level. Then, without even realizing it, we often rely on those strengths even more. We turn the knob bit by bit and, unknowingly, make it less likely to achieve the results we really want. And worst of all, we run the risk of damaging relationships along the way. Consider the table below as an example of how strengths can start working against us if we have the volume turned too high:

STRENGTH	WHEN THE VOLUME IS TURNED TOO HIGH
Being **methodical.** You accomplish your work in a systematic, efficient, and disciplined way.	Being **inactive.** You get trapped in analysis paralysis, slowing momentum until it becomes inoperable. Those around you get frustrated by the lack of progress.
Being **practical.** You focus on empirical solutions that are effective and efficient.	Being **pessimistic.** You can always find a reason for *not* doing something. You're viewed as a naysayer and not seen as one who can lead, inspire, or motivate others.

STRENGTH	WHEN THE VOLUME IS TURNED TOO HIGH
Being **efficient.** You are organized, competent, and minimize waste.	Being **inflexible.** You shut yourself off from the input of those around you in your desire to get things done. Your colleagues feel like you don't trust them or value their perspective. As a result, you lose their creative energy and miss out on unanticipated discoveries and solutions.
Being **open-minded.** You're willing to consider new ideas in an unprejudiced and a nonjudgmental fashion.	Being **weak-willed.** It becomes easier to surrender your principles and agree with the last person you heard, even though you see it differently. You're less likely to stick to the solutions, plans, and decisions you believe in. People won't respect you, knowing you'll always give in.
Being **loyal.** You're consistent in your support and allegiance to others.	Being **gullible.** You may choose to overlook flagrant problems or flaws that negatively impact the relationship or situation. You ignore red flags in others and exacerbate your own blind spots.
Being **accommodating.** You're adaptable and considerate of the thoughts and opinions of others.	Being **overly involved** in everyone else's problems. You easily get stretched too thin and risk burnout, while more important things fall by the wayside. The quality of everything suffers—instead of doing a few important things well, you marginally impact a host of mediocre things.
Being **passionate.** You're energized by ardent feelings and strong beliefs.	Being **exhausting.** Your zeal and energy turns into impatience. You start stepping on toes and crossing boundaries, believing that others don't care as much as you do. Being always frenzied, you dilute everything.

STRENGTH	WHEN THE VOLUME IS TURNED TOO HIGH
Being **confident.** You're assertive and self-reliant, with a poise that positively motivates others.	Being **arrogant.** Instead of inspiring trust and loyalty, you come across as exaggerated and focused on your own sense of self-importance and superiority. People feel distrusted and, therefore, become disengaged and uninspired.
Being **decisive.** You make decisions quickly and effectively.	Being **reckless.** You proceed before you have the necessary information, acting rashly and putting people and projects at risk. As a result, your colleagues feel that their input isn't heard and may stop participating or being engaged. You make commitments prematurely, some of which you can't or shouldn't keep.
Being a **visionary.** You plan the future with imagination and wisdom.	Being a **dreamer.** While a visionary acts, a dreamer is content with the dreaming itself—and action falls by the wayside.
Being **assertive.** You're forthright and confident, making bold and decisive decisions when called for.	Being **domineering.** You assert your will over others in an arrogant and often demeaning way.

Prior to FranklinCovey, I worked with Matt. He was an extraordinarily talented individual with two degrees in his field. Matt had many strengths, but he was especially known for his drive to get high-quality results. Efficient and organized, Matt should have been on the fast track for senior management. Instead, his career stalled. Each time a high-profile project surfaced, it was invariably awarded to somebody else on Matt's team—often to those who were less skilled and educated than he was. And while he was the kind of person who kept his emotions in check, I wondered if the constant string of disappointments was wearing him down.

To my surprise, one day Matt asked if I would be willing to give him some honest feedback. I was happy to help. He expressed his growing frustration that he wasn't being asked to work on the larger, more visible projects. It was a small company at the time, so I knew that Matt had a reputation for being somewhat difficult to work with—that his strengths of focus and drive were sometimes perceived as being rigid, demanding, and overly negative. The most successful team members I've worked with not only have superb skills and experience, but also have a spirit of engagement, enthusiasm, and general positivity. These skills didn't come to mind when working with Matt. I struggled with a way to share this feedback without being hurtful. It's one thing to say, "You might need more experience," or "Maybe you could work on a particular skill." It's another to say, "People just don't like working with you." But since Matt had approached me and I really wanted to help, I shared my perspective. I was deliberate about offering specific examples so that he could see the unintended outcome of what I believed was a strength dialed up too high.

I reminded him of the time we were brainstorming solutions to a client problem in a team meeting. Instead of acknowledging each of the ideas, when Matt didn't agree with some of the suggestions, he would say, "That will never work," shutting down the enthusiasm for the idea-generating process. I reiterated as to how smart and savvy he was, but that the volume of his efficiency strength left the impression that he wanted to be the lone genius and leave everyone behind. I also shared a couple of emails he'd sent in which his language was abrupt—bordering on harsh. "I am just trying to be respectful of people's time and make sure we get the results as fast as we can," Matt said. After a few minutes together, I realized Matt was completely unaware that his style and approach (turned up too high) had created a negative reputation.

We then talked about what people do when they feel shut down or left behind. They stop engaging. And while his idea, in many cases, turned out to be the right one, shutting down the input of others was jeopardizing his effectiveness. We also talked about how a few tweaks in his word choices could shift the tone of his emails from abrupt and harsh to friendly and collaborative.

Matt then really impressed me. Instead of taking offense or feeling hurt, he began looking for opportunities to implement the ideas we had discussed. And while efficiency was an important strength for him to not lose, he dialed it back so he could take the time to soften his approach, acknowledging and encouraging the contribution of others. Before long, I heard some of his co-workers take notice: "I was pleasantly surprised when Matt validated my idea rather than shutting it down in the meeting yesterday," or "Wow! Matt heard me out and liked my suggestion."

Little by little, Matt started seeing that his projects moved forward more effectively because of his focus on relationships. As a result, he started naturally dialing back the volume on the strengths that were getting in the way before. Best of all, we no longer had to walk on eggshells, worried if Matt was going to shut down the energy of the team. Matt found himself being invited to more project teams and getting his career back on track.

Like many of us, Matt hadn't realized he'd been turning the volume up too high on one of his particular strengths. His intentions had always been good, and it was easy to rely on the strengths that had served him well in the past. In my own case, I have an amazing, world-renowned strength for humility. Just kidding. But I do believe I have the strength of being accommodating. Like many of our strengths, it's something that's been a part of me my entire life. Now, that might seem like a pretty good thing all in all, and you might wonder how being accommodating can lead you down a path you don't like, but too much accommodation can pull you into situations where you feel responsible for things and people you probably shouldn't. You end up trying to help everyone, everywhere, and sometimes at a tremendous personal cost. In the middle of writing this book, in addition to doing my full-time job, I was asked to deliver a last-minute keynote speech as a favor to a colleague who had a work crisis. A request like this one can be stressful because of the preparation required: I'd lose a good deal of time on writing this book, I would still have all of my regular responsibilities, and I'd want to keep honoring my family commitments. Immediately, my mind screams, *No way, Todd! You're slammed as it is. You can't do everything!* I want to accommodate her need of getting this keynote off her calendar. I'm also invested in her solving the work crisis; I want to be helpful and I care.

My accommodation strength begins to take over, and because it's one of my go-to strengths, I let it. As my mind continues to pull the fire alarm, my mouth opens, and I utter, "Sure, I'll do it." I then literally start doing the math in my head: *If I cut my sleep down to five hours a night, I can probably squeeze this in. I can also reschedule my weekend plans, just to be sure.* But like my son leaving the volume too high on the car stereo, I don't consider the impact of my decision on the people around me. I will add an extra burden to the book-project team because I'm not available on the days to which I had originally committed. And while I think I'll be able to save my weekend, all it will take is one unexpected work issue, or me miscalculating my time, and my family will bear the cost of my overdone accommodation strength. And worse, when the volume is turned up too high, everything suffers: I get less than stellar results on the book, deliver a less than engaging keynote presentation, and have less than optimal relationships with the people who matter most.

No one dials up the volume of their strengths with the intention of a bad outcome. Yet, it happens. If the volume of our strengths is set too high, turning it down can often make our strengths more effective. I recognize this approach may seem counterintuitive. We're used to mantras such as bear down, work harder, push through it! And while those all have their place, there's wisdom in knowing when to lighten up, to take a step back, or to just say no. In my own case, I could have declined the keynote invitation by explaining the pressures I was also under, yet stay true to my strength by helping my colleague find an equally capable replacement. Had I done that, I would have been faithful to all my relationships while still being accommodating. I would also have had the time to write the chapter "Synchronized Swimming and Its Parallels to Strategic Planning," but regrettably, I had to cut something.

To be fair, we may be unwittingly encouraging people to dial up their strengths. Many of the tools used to measure strengths send mixed messages regarding this point. Consider the numerous 360-degree surveys that rank strengths and propose that the higher you score, the better you're doing. It seems like a reasonable premise on the surface, but researchers Bob Kaplan and Rob Kaiser found a problem. "Such tools overlook a key lesson from decades of research on derailment: More is not always better, and executives lose their jobs when their strengths become weaknesses through overuse."[11] Be suspicious of any strengths-measuring instrument having an inherent premise that more is better.

THE RIGHT VENUE

Earlier in this section, I suggested you think of deploying your strengths like a musician on a stage. I shared the risks of raising the volume because we grow too accustomed to the current level, or cranking up the volume under the assumption that more is better. But in keeping with our analogy, we should also consider the venue in which we're performing; that is, sometimes getting the volume right means choosing another go-to strength or recognizing that the venue or situation is calling for a different strength altogether—one that may not be as natural to you and may need to be developed.

A good friend of mine told me the story of a CEO he worked for. This entrepreneurial man's strength was his ability to focus and get quick results. When the company first began, it was obvious how accomplished he was on his own, delivering keynotes at large conferences and pumping out articles, blogs, and several books at a steady pace. He had great skills for a startup company. Yet, when his company started growing, adding additional talent and personalities, this dialed-up strength started to work against him. It manifested itself as a palpable impatience for any errors, glitches, or snags, which then surfaced as a tendency to micromanage people and processes. He would often excuse his behavior as him being simply who he was, and his style necessary to growing the business. "Hey, look, we are where we are today because of quick turnaround and quick decision making," he would say, and gave himself permission to turn up the volume even higher.

He required that his team be innovative, but then challenged the process when it didn't yield immediate results. Within a few years, turnover began to increase with both new and seasoned employees. People in the organization who stayed learned that the best way to keep the CEO off their backs was to appear busy, even if they weren't, being careful not to make a noticeable mistake. One needed to generate an activity-laden scorecard and appear to do a great deal of work at a near-frantic pace to please him. Employee engagement waned. Unfortunately, the CEO was unable or unwilling to acknowledge the change of venue: from a startup to a rapidly growing business. While the old venue needed a high degree of his independent focus and quick agility, the growing company required much more interdependence—purposefully seeking others' ideas and patience to work through the inevitable glitches and snags that come with involving additional people. Relationships with many of the talented team members began to fracture. Those who were incapable or simply unwilling to look busy for its own sake, or who needed a safer, more encouraging environment in which to unlock their best stuff, started to disengage. Today many of his original team members no longer work for him, and the company is losing market share.

We have many venues in our lives, not the least of which is moving from work to home. We should be especially careful that the strengths that serve us in our career are not assumed to be the same ones needed by our family and significant others, and vice versa. An important part of getting the volume right isn't just about turning our strengths down when necessary, but making sure we have the right strength applied at the right time and in the right situation. I wondered if my golfer friend Thomas might be making the same kind of mistake . . . .

● ● ●

It took nearly twenty minutes before we made it to the tee box. The teenager at the pro shop did his best to shuffle the schedule and squeeze us in. Thomas thanked him, missing the annoyed glances from the others who had showed up on time. As I pulled my driver from the bag, I noticed a pair of golfers who were waiting for us, arms crossed and glaring.

"It's worth the time it takes to do things right," Thomas announced as he prepared for his swing. "You'll see."

Thomas always had a methodical nature, and he seemed to enjoy the analytical process. I'm sure that's what made him a good programmer. But I also wondered if he'd lost track of how far he'd turned the volume up on that particular strength. I motioned to the golfers behind us and invited them to play through. Thomas tossed me an inquisitive look as we stepped off the tee and allowed the other players to move ahead.

"What was that all about?" Thomas asked.

"I don't think I could have concentrated knowing those guys were waiting for us the entire time."

"I understand," Thomas said. "You're uncomfortable making people wait. I suppose I'm not, something my partners would probably tell you as well."

"You mean your call from earlier?" I asked.

"Yeah. They're upset that I want to delay the product launch. They don't understand that we need the time to make sure everything's right." It sounded reasonable, but I wondered if what I was experiencing on the golf course was similar to what Thomas's partners were going through.

"So, what does right look like in your world?" I asked. "I mean, I get software updates all the time. Is there a point where you ever get it totally right?"

"You sound like the marketing team," Thomas replied. "And I suppose there's some truth in that. While software is always changing, in our effort to keep up, we can't jeopardize the quality. But marketing is bugged because they're missing deadlines."

"Because you're slowing it down to get it right?" I responded.

"Yes," Thomas agreed. "But I don't think the deadline should prevent us from at least trying to get quality as high as possible."

"So how do you balance things?" I asked. "You know, the need to be agile in your development, meet the launch deadlines, and yet make sure you have all the quality assurance taken care of?"

"You prioritize. And for me, it's always going to be quality assurance that wins out, even if it means missing a launch window. Or three."

"Three?" I practically gasped. I wasn't an expert in the technology field, but I'd served with enough companies to know regularly missing product launches could have serious consequences.

"I know. Three delays make for bad business," Thomas confessed.

"Hey please don't be offended by this. I know being detail-oriented is a strength of yours—something I've always admired. I mean, look at your clubs. You could practically eat off one of those things they're so clean."

"I'll take that as a compliment," Thomas said with a smile.

"And yet we ended up being late for our tee time," I continued, "which in turn affected the other golfers who had showed up on time. So I'm wondering if you have that particular strength of yours dialed up so high you're missing some of the bigger picture."

"So you're suggesting there's some room for compromise with my partners?"

"I'm not a programmer by any stretch of the imagination, but the practice is sound. I've been in situations where people need to step back at times and make sure their strengths are actually working for them and not getting in the way."

"Well, I'll give that some thought." Thomas said as we took our places on the tee.

On the drive home, I wondered about where I'd set the volume on my own strengths—especially the one about accommodating others. I decided to make a mental list and reprioritize some of my upcoming commitments so that I could focus quality time on a few important things rather than try to do everything. By the way, polishing my golf clubs wasn't on that list.

APPLICATION 11

GET YOUR VOLUME RIGHT

1. Identify three of your top go-to strengths.

2. Describe what it might look like and the impact it would have if you were to set the volume too high on each of these strengths.

3. Ask a trusted friend or colleague if he or she has ever seen you exhibit any of the behaviors you identified below. If so, ask that person to describe the situation and the impact of your dialed-up strength.

4. Identify a different strength that might have been more effective in the situation and/or which ways you might turn the volume down on the original strength in the future.

YOUR GO-TO STRENGTH	IMPACT IF VOLUME IS TOO HIGH	SITUATION AND IMPACT WHEN VOLUME IS SET TOO HIGH	NEW STRENGTH NEEDED OR WAYS TO DIAL DOWN STRENGTH
Being proactive.	Overstepping boundaries.	Last week's team meeting. Lori was offended I took over her job.	Seek understanding before jumping in.

EXTEND TRUST

ARE YOU MORE INCLINED TO INITIALLY DISTRUST OTHERS THAN TO TRUST THEM?

If so, you may want to consider

PRACTICE 12: EXTEND TRUST.

When you don't extend trust, your room may feel like Sartre's hell because:

- You lose the passion and engagement of others.
- You're convinced you need to micromanage everything and, therefore, lose valuable time.
- You limit possibilities and minimize opportunities for great relationships at work and home.

Rick was the vice president of marketing for a medium-size technology company, and had just received approval to make a short video to highlight the key features and benefits of their latest product. He contacted a friend of his who had produced a number of award-winning videos in his organization, and was given the name of a local production company his friend highly recommended. Rick invited Alyssa, his senior marketing manager, to reach out to the vendor, sharing the project's scope and budget. The vendor responded positively that they could accomplish what Rick needed, and sent samples of their work.

"These guys are really good," Alyssa announced at their weekly team meeting. She had sent the examples to the team so everyone had a chance to review their work. "Did you notice all the awards they've won?"

"Plus, they know our budget and are willing to work within it," another of Rick's team members added. But Rick was hesitant.

"I'm just not sure," Rick announced. His team was a bit perplexed by his reaction.

"Is there some criterion they're falling short on?" Alyssa asked.

"Not really," Rick answered. "It's just important that we get it right."

"How about we get some references from former clients?" another team member asked. Rick agreed, and Alyssa sent the request. Over the next week, they received numerous reviews from a variety of clients, all of whom spoke highly of the production team and their work. Rick remained hesitant, however.

"I'm just not there yet," he told his team.

Wondering if the issue was around the price, Alyssa proposed a budget that was slightly lower than the vendor's standard rate, suggesting that it would be a way to earn trust and future business. The vendor agreed to make the concession in good faith, but when Rick was given the news, he still remained unconvinced.

"We're starting to push up against our production deadline," Alyssa told him.

"I understand. Are there more examples I can look at?"

"Um, I'm sure there are . . ."

"And why don't you talk to a few more customers while you're at it," Rick continued.

With the deadline looming, Alyssa returned to her office. She stared at her computer, having a difficult time composing the next email to the vendor. "We've seen their work, we've heard from their clients, and they've reduced their price. So, what in the world is Rick waiting for?"

• • •

If you recall from the "Take Stock of Your Emotional Bank Accounts" practice, trust is the ultimate outcome of investing in others. In the "Behave Your Way to Credibility" practice, we learned that high character and competence are essential for realizing trust. Simply put, when it comes to relationships, trust matters. In fact, it's essential. This practice is not only about trust being a *belief* in someone, it's also about putting that belief into *action*. Trust, to be fully realized, must be extended to others.

If you chart trust as a continuum, on one extreme is distrust and suspicion. Here, you find Rick, who requires people to go overboard proving themselves before he'll even consider giving up control or moving forward. On the other side is blind trust and gullibility. Here, you find people like my aunt who almost gave an anonymous caller her Social Security number in order to receive the Mediterranean cruise, new car, and amazing spending account she'd just won. (Fortunately, my niece overheard the call and intercepted before any damage was done.)

DISTRUST/ SUSPICION — **BLIND TRUST/ GULLIBILITY**

While occasionally, some of us teeter on either extreme, most of us land somewhere in the middle. But from watching and coaching people over the past few decades, I've concluded that the majority of relationship snags are rarely caused by people trusting too much; they're caused by people trusting too little.

Many factors contribute to people being distrustful of others. We may have learned to be suspicious because of our family of origin.

Maybe our cultural and social conditioning gave us reasons to mistrust. For instance, a good friend of mine grew up learning to mistrust others as a general rule. One day in the car with her parents and two sisters, her mother announced, "The only people you can trust in the world are in the car right now. Never forget that." My friend has spent most of her life trying to overcome that original conditioning. Certainly, what we hear, read, or watch can breed more fear than trust, and can work to shut down a natural, trusting heart.

My experience leads me to believe that the most common reason we mistrust is because of past negative experiences. It's usually life's emotional trip-ups that cause us to withhold our trust. When my friend Kurt was five years old, he was in his backyard playing with a neighbor's new dog. In his enthusiasm, Kurt pulled too hard on the dog's collar, hurting and startling the dog. This action caused the dog to lunge toward Kurt and bite him on the face. Terrified by the sudden turn of events, Kurt ran home screaming and bleeding. His mom rushed him to the emergency room where he later left with fifteen stitches and a big bruise under his right eye. As a result of that highly impactful and negative experience, Kurt adopted a strong belief: *All dogs are dangerous and shouldn't be trusted*. From that day forward, Kurt avoided all dogs. And even though he knows his belief isn't universally true, at fifty-eight years old today, he still avoids eye contact with a teacup poodle.

THE CONSEQUENCES OF NOT EXTENDING TRUST

How many of us have adopted similar beliefs to Kurt's—only with people? Perhaps you've been burned in a previous job by a boss or business partner, or had a terrible experience in a past relationship. Or maybe you just get overwhelmed by the constant stories in the news about the corruption around the globe. Perhaps, like Kurt, you have concluded that it isn't safe to trust. Regardless of the reason, once we develop a suspicious worldview (especially one that originated in a strong emotional experience), we tend to look at everything through that lens. If someone has burned us in the past, it's easy to jump to the conclusion that no one should be trusted. It can negatively color our perceptions when we meet someone new, and if the propensity *not* to trust runs deep, it may justify our ongoing disassociation and mistrust of people and their motives. Of course, maintaining an element of caution is vital to living safely and securely. Living at either end of the trust continuum can make life difficult for ourselves and those around us.

Abraham Lincoln said, "If you trust, you will be disappointed occasionally, but if you mistrust, you will be miserable all the time." This maxim proved true for Don, a manager I worked with a few years ago, who spent a tremendous amount of time and energy hiring two writers to accommodate the department's ever-growing product demands. Within six months, it was obvious that neither person had the aptitude necessary for the job, and he had to let them go. Investing in these newly hired people for several months at a critical time in the business caused a great deal of emotional upheaval for him and his team, as well as significant productivity loss.

Stung by the experience, Don started to be suspicious of every candidate he interviewed thereafter, and thus became so concerned about vetting for the perfect hire that he went outside of the standard hiring practices employed by the company. Assuming that more opinions would alleviate mistakes, he made every potential candidate go through several rounds of interviews, on top of the three rounds of interviews already conducted by the recruiting team.

While there were reasons for Don's mistrust, his suspicion of all candidates and the recruitment process came at a high cost. The additional interviews increased the length of the hiring process by several months. He lost many well-qualified candidates because they received other offers, and the lack of staff resulted in missing critical deadlines.

When it came to my attention that several positions in his department had been open for over six months, I met with Don to have a transparent conversation. "I know you're aware that you're short-staffed and it's impacting other areas of the company that are dependent on your production. I'd like to share something with you that may help. Given your recent experience with two hires not working out, I understand your reluctance to use our existing recruitment and vetting processes. But may I share with you a little bit more about how our recruitment teams screen candidates before they ever get to you?"

I went on to explain the rigorous process already in place and how it had yielded some of our best talent. As he listened to me explain the thorough vetting process, I could see him starting to feel more comfortable. By the end of our conversation, he agreed to follow the process others were using. More important, he saw that by not extending trust, he was slowing things down; and his team, and those who depended on them, were paying the price. He realized that if he hired faster, he could also identify and replace any mismatched hires more quickly, if needed.

No matter how hard we try, sometimes people just don't work out. And because we're all human, we're bound to disappoint each other occasionally. However, when we lead with suspicion, we automatically put the relationship at a disadvantage, either stunting its potential or abandoning it altogether. If you want a glimpse into Sartre's hell, consider an eternity surrounded by people who never learn to trust each other.

THE BENEFITS OF EXTENDING TRUST

Sierra had worked for two years in her organization's human resources department. In their regular one-on-one meeting, Sierra's boss, Janeen, told Sierra how much potential she saw in her. She committed to mentor Sierra and give her the experiences she needed to advance her career. Elated by the vote of confidence, Sierra rose to the occasion; she did everything she could to live up to her boss's expectations.

For the next several months, Janeen was a great ally. She continued to extend trust to Sierra, increasing her responsibilities and visibility in the organization. Janeen and other members of the leadership team soon began to see Sierra as a viable candidate, should Janeen retire or be promoted.

After a few years of working together, Janeen confided in Sierra during one of their weekly meetings, "I learned a big lesson last week, and I think you could benefit from hearing about it. If you can learn from my mistake and avoid making a similar one, I think you'd be the better for it." Janeen went on to share that she had overestimated her ability to prepare several new reports for the annual board of directors meeting the week before. She'd assumed (incorrectly, as it turned out) that her years of experience would allow her to absorb the data the new reports needed to include. So instead of prioritizing this critical task, she figured her smarts would save the day, and allowed less important, pressing matters to stand in the way of allocating sufficient preparation time. As a result, not only were the reports late, but they weren't completely accurate and lacked the level of detail the board required. Janeen's poor judgment put her boss, the CEO, in a very awkward situation. He pulled Janeen aside and gave her an earful after the meeting.

"This is a difficult mistake for me to admit," she continued. "I shouldn't have been so cavalier about preparing those reports. I should have taken the time to understand just how much work was involved. But I'm hoping you can learn from it and never find yourself in a similar situation."

Sierra was surprised—and impressed. Her boss had been transparent and vulnerable. Janeen wasn't obligated to share this information or extend this type of trust to her, but she did. Sierra's respect for Janeen increased substantially that day. She learned from Janeen that not only was it safe to make mistakes under her leadership, but that Janeen's trust was strong enough to allow her to admit a mistake to help Sierra grow.

Loyalty can't exist without trust. Sue, a colleague and good friend of mine, wrote about this principle in her book *The Ultimate Competitive Advantage*.[12] When she was a key executive in the McDonald's Corporation, she met often with Ray Kroc, its founder. She recounted the following story to me: "There were times that Ray couldn't pay his suppliers within the thirty-day window. Cash flow was always an issue in the early days of building the Golden Arches into a global brand. So Ray sat down with a key soft-drink supplier and explained that he may sometimes be late with a payment, but promised he would always pay, which he did.

"The abundant way the soft-drink company responded created a deep loyalty in Ray. He promised them he would never change providers. They shook hands on the deal. And to this day, McDonald's remains with the company. I learned about the extent of his loyalty personally when I was driving with Ray. He found a package of competing soda in my car. He explained how important that handshake deal had been to him—how helpful their long-standing provider had been when he was struggling to keep the business alive.

"He then asked me how I could possibly buy something from a competitor. When I explained that I enjoyed the somewhat sweeter taste, he smiled and said there must be something wrong with my taste buds. Not long after, a delivery truck pulled up in front of my Chicago apartment to deliver a year's supply of a foreign version of the vendor's drinks, with multiple bows and a big card from Ray that read, 'The European formula is sweeter than the U.S. formula. No excuses, Sue. Ask for more when you need it. We are loyal to our partners, and I am loyal to you.' By trusting Ray Kroc, the soft-drink company gained its largest and most profitable customer forever."

HOW TO EXTEND TRUST

So how do you know whether or not you should extend trust? In my experience, the best approach is always to start with a high propensity to trust, then follow it up with three quick assessments. It's a combination of using both your head and your heart.

1. **Assess the situation.** First, identify and consider what you're trusting the person to do: To deliver a weekly report to you on time? To win an important legal case? To sell software? To build a rocket? To honor and cherish you until death do you part?

2. **Assess the risk.** Second, assess the potential risks: What happens if the person to whom you've extended trust fails, underperforms, gives up, gets distracted, or missteps? Are the stakes for failure high, or can you tolerate a learning curve? Be realistic and objective here.

3. **Assess the credibility.** Finally, assess the character and competence of the person to whom you're extending trust. Do you trust that person to be honest and follow through (character)? Does he or she have the experience or skillset necessary for the task at hand (competence)? If not, does the person have the discipline and drive to grow into it?

Once you've made the three assessments, you can better determine where your trust should fall on the trust continuum:

- If the risk is relatively low and the credibility of the person is high, by all means, extend trust.

- If the risk is high and the credibility is low, you may need to slow down the process, modify your plan, and work with the person to increase his or her skills before you extend trust. In some cases, even when the credibility is solid, the risk may be too high to immediately extend trust.

You'll want to make these assessments as quickly as possible so that you avoid any risk of extending trust in a situation that doesn't warrant it. For instance, we recently hired someone in our creative-services division with the expectation that he would mentor others in several state-of-the-art graphic-design programs. Within a month, we realized that, while he knew the programs peripherally, he wasn't nearly as proficient with them as we needed him to be. While he had good character, we hadn't done our due diligence to assess the risk thoroughly enough. We overestimated what we assumed were advanced skills in specific design programs. We ended up wasting valuable time and resources finding a new role for him and replacing him with other talent.

The better we assess, the less likely we will misplace our trust. But absent significant reasons for holding back, there are benefits for having a propensity to trust versus to distrust. Consider the story of Maria. After moving from her native country, Colombia, she was hired as a receptionist in one branch of a large auto dealership and had no education or training past high school. As the weeks went by, Maria started coming in late to work. Larry, her boss, decided to speak with her and find out why. He learned that Maria enjoyed her job and working with people, but she was a single mother who needed to drop her kids off at day care before starting the work day. She told him it wasn't an excuse, but getting the children ready each morning could cause delays in her schedule. She committed that she would find a way to make it work. So Larry decided to extend her his trust: "I believe in you," he told her. "You have talent, and you're good with the public. But I need you to be here. If you continue to be late, I'll need to let you go. But if you show up consistently on time in the future, I promise I will help you make a career here."

Before he made any decision, Larry took the time to assess the situation. Rather than simply issue her a warning, he sat down with her to better understand what was going on. By doing so, he learned a bit more about Maria and her challenges. He also considered the risks: Given the nature of the job, there were likely many candidates who could fill the role. If he extended trust and she was late again, it wouldn't bring the organization down. It was important that she show up on time, but the consequences for not doing so were minimal. Finally, Larry assessed Maria's character and competence. He learned she was motivated to keep her job and provide for her children, but she also didn't try to excuse her tardiness. She had committed to figure it out, which said a lot about who she was and her confidence in her abilities.

Maria made some changes with her morning routine and showed up the next day on time. She was never late again. Larry took note of her dedication and how skillfully she interacted with customers to build rapport. He knew his trust hadn't been misplaced, and he suspected there was even more that Maria could do. After several months, she asked him to consider her for a promotion in the customer-advocacy department. Even though she was a good worker, the differences between her previous job and this new, more demanding environment might be too much of a struggle for her.

Larry took time to assess again. While she may not have had the depth of understanding or knowledge about how to resolve the types of customer complaints that would be necessary in the new job, he knew other employees were willing to mentor her. And while her lack of experience put her at a disadvantage from her peers, he had plenty of evidence that she was a quick learner and skillful when dealing with people. He committed to provide a safe environment in which she could make mistakes and learn. Maria took off! It was the exact right fit, and she far exceeded everyone's expectations. She eventually became the manager of the entire customer-advocacy department.

Now, you probably think that's the end of the story, but it's not. When a position became available in Maria's department, she recommended Jose, a young high-school graduate who had no training. Like Larry had done with her, she considered the young man's credibility. Despite his lack of experience, she sensed his willingness to learn and knew from references that he had a terrific work ethic. Like Maria, Jose excelled! She ultimately hired him as her executive assistant, paying it forward.

Extending trust is a matter of the head and the heart. While you start with a high propensity to trust, you must follow it up with a diligent assessment of the credibility of the person to determine whether or not to extend trust.

WHAT TO DO IF SOMEONE WON'T EXTEND TRUST TO YOU

Sometimes no matter how hard you try, you can't prove yourself to someone who withholds trust. While you can't change someone's propensity to trust or distrust, you can certainly influence it. You can invite the person to extend trust by proactively working to increase your own credibility—your character and competence. (See "Practice 3: Behave Your Way to Credibility.")

An entrepreneurial friend of mine, Alan, started his own business in an office that consisted of a card table and a bedsheet hanging over his basement window. He had the chance to become a vendor for a large technology company. Alan proposed he produce the company's multimedia sales training, but he had little credibility in the eyes of the company's vice president.

"Have you ever worked with a company our size?" the VP asked my friend on a call a mutual acquaintance had set up.

"No, sir, not yet," Alan replied.

"Have you had experience developing sales training for our industry?"

"Not yet," Alan said. You can imagine how the rest of the conversation went. My friend was hoping the organization would trust him to take on a significant project, but the odds of the vice president making the switch were about zero to none. Alan realized that he needed to prove himself and show that he had the competence to help their organization.

"Do you perhaps have a smaller project I could take on for you?" Alan asked the vice president. "Something low-risk? I'd cut my fees to simply cover the costs. I'm confident that if you give me a chance, you'll be thrilled with what I produce."

The vice president was intrigued, and since the risk (and expense) was low, he decided to give Alan the opportunity. Alan poured his time and talents into making a twenty-minute training video unlike any the company had ever seen before. The vice president was impressed and invited my friend to take on a slightly larger project. And so it went, bit by bit, Alan proving his competence and character along the way. In fewer than six months, the vice president signed a large and exclusive contract, placing his trust completely with my friend and his fledgling company. (Things went so well, Alan went out and bought a new card table.)

Sometimes, earning trust takes a dogged determination to prove your credibility one small step at a time. If you find yourself in such a situation, don't be afraid to schedule a conversation with the individual from whom you need trust. Simply ask, "What do you need to see from me to earn your trust?" And while this may seem obvious, it's often so obvious that we fail to do it. Once you're clear on the other

person's expectations, follow through on modeling the identified behaviors and check in regularly. You can often earn someone's trust if
you're willing to invest in the process.

There's risk in everything. Even after thoroughly assessing, you
can get burned by people to whom you've extended great trust. It's
happened to me on occasion and it hurts. But I still believe there's so
much more to be gained by leading with trust over suspicion. It was
the lesson Rick and his marketing team were about to learn.

● ● ●

*With the deadline looming, the senior manager returned to her office. She
stared at her computer, having a difficult time composing the next email to the
vendor. "We've seen their work, we've heard from their clients, and they've
reduced their price. So, what in the world is Rick waiting for?"*

*During the next team meeting, the senior manager shared the update with
the marketing team. "As Rick requested, the vendor sent us more examples
and names of clients for us to talk to. I've received the same feedback from
the latest clients, all of whom were pleased with the work and would hire
the vendor again." She paused, swallowing and looking slightly embarrassed.
"Rick also asked me to push on their latest bid and reduce the amount by four
hundred dollars."*

"Aren't we past the project's start date?" one of the team members asked.

*"Technically, yes," Rick interjected, "but I'm sure once we've made a deci-
sion, they can make the time up."*

*"Well, maybe not . . ." the senior sales manager added. All eyes turned
to her.*

"Is there a problem?" Rick asked.

*The senior manager looked down at her cellphone. "I just got word . . .
the vendor's been booked for a large project and won't be available for four to
five months."*

*"Four to five months?" Rick repeated. "We can't possibly wait that
long."*

There was an awkward silence as the team members stared at each other from around the table. The entire deadline was now at risk, and the marketing department's reputation was likely to get a black eye. Rick sighed, "And here I was, almost ready to pull the trigger. Now you see why I have a hard time trusting people!"

APPLICATION 12

EXTEND TRUST

1. **Identify a person or situation in which you need to extend trust.** For example, hiring a new vendor, giving a new responsibility to a child, putting together a new project team, delegating assignments while you're on vacation.

2. **Assess the situation.** Describe what you are trusting the person with (see examples below).

   - If hiring a vendor: to build a client-management system according to specs by December.

   - If giving responsibility to a child: to clean the bedroom and make the bed every day.

   - If putting together a new project team: to work collaboratively to develop an internal communications strategy by the time of the merger.

   - If delegating assignments while on vacation: to conduct a follow-up meeting with an important client and secure next year's subscription.

3. **Assess the risk.** Describe the visibility and importance of each of the possible outcomes.

4. **Assess the credibility of the person involved.** What is the level of his or her character and competence?

MAKE IT SAFE TO TELL THE TRUTH

WHEN WAS THE LAST TIME YOU RECEIVED FEEDBACK FROM SOMEONE?

If you can't remember, you may want to consider

PRACTICE 13: MAKE IT SAFE TO TELL THE TRUTH.

When you don't make it safe to tell the truth, your room may feel like Sartre's hell because:

- You're unaware of what you don't know, likely missing key insights about your impact on others and the chance to change it if necessary.
- You have less rapport with others, missing out on deep and trusted relationships.
- You not only discover that the emperor has no clothes, but the emperor could be you.

Meg is a friend of mine and HR director for a large medical-parts manufac-
turing plant. She recently shared a challenging work situation with me that
occurred a few months ago. Several people on the front lines were complain-
ing to her about their senior manager, Carsten. "He was overly directive in
his style and didn't listen to their ideas. The fact that many of the work-
ers came from other countries and spoke several different languages made
it more difficult for them to communicate with Carsten. In addition, there
were about a hundred people for every manager on the plant floor. The team
meetings amounted to people sitting with their mouths shut while one of
Carsten's managers reiterated how Carsten wanted things done."

"How did that work for him?" I joked.

She went on to explain that, to Carsten, his methods seemed perfectly
appropriate. As the head engineer and lead manager, he felt it was up to
him to have all the answers—that leaders like him should give feedback,
not take it. Meg said, "I suspected he felt that being open to feedback might
make him seem weak and confirm his belief that true leaders aren't supposed
to be vulnerable.

"It's like he was wearing a T-shirt that said, 'There's nothing you can
tell me that I don't already know.' He ignored any of my attempts to give
him insight on what he might do better." She sighed.

"Sounds like a difficult coaching challenge for you," I commiserated.

"But here is the worst part," she continued. "The plant was suffering
from significant quality-control problems. Ten out of every hundred seals on
the tubing kits were defective, and the failure rate was rapidly increasing.
The workers were trying to give Carsten feedback on why the error rate was
so high, but he didn't want to hear it."

"So, what did you do?" I asked.

● ● ●

Many of you can relate: you have important feedback for someone but
are afraid or hesitant to give it because you know the person won't
take it well. And I suspect that, in some circumstances, some of you
can also relate to Carsten, the person who avoids feedback or who is

unwilling to receive it because it makes him or her feel vulnerable. Take an honest moment and ask yourself, "Do I make it safe for others to tell me the truth?"

Let's go back to Sartre's play in the introduction. Not only is each room filled with people we don't like, but the windows are bricked up, the lights are on constantly, and there are no mirrors. Even if people wanted to, there is no way for them to take an honest look at themselves. People are so busy looking for ways to change others, that they forget to ask how they might change themselves. Like many of us, they neglect to ask for the type of feedback that will help them get better.

Why do we resist feedback? Why don't we have the courage to ask for it in the first place? For most of us, setting ourselves up to receive what we see as criticism is unpleasant at best, and confidence-deflating at worst. So we choose not to create opportunities for what we assume will be negative feedback from others. We all know how hard it is to give ourselves feedback (that is, to step on the bathroom scale), but it can be overwhelming, even paralyzing, to get it from someone else. As humans, we are vulnerable. It's the very thing that makes us human. Feedback from others—whether it's 100 percent accurate or not—brings to the surface what we don't want to admit: that each of us is a work in progress in at least some areas.

To prepare us for this practice, it might be helpful to note the origin of the word *feedback*. The two words, *feed* (v.) and *back* (adv.), help uncover what the goal of feedback should always be. *Feed* comes from the Old English *fedan*, which means to "nourish, sustain, and foster." The meaning of *back* includes "to support," and is the basis of words like *backed* and *backing* today. If we see feedback as something useful that can support our process of getting better, perhaps we won't be so threatened by it. We may even look for ways to invite it in. Granted, not all feedback is given with the intent to support or help us; we need to be discerning about the feedback we allow in. The best type of feedback has the goal or intent of fostering our growth. Knowing how to receive feedback and when to invite it in, or respectfully hear it but choose no action, requires careful self-examination.

Self-awareness, or the ability to think about one's thinking, is one of the greatest of our human gifts. It allows us to examine our motives and actions and decide if they're aligned with who we really want to be and, if not, to self-correct. But self-awareness is not just about examining ourselves. It's also about recognizing that we have blind spots (see "Practice 11: Get Your Volume Right") and considering others' perspectives. You'll recall one of the reasons in Sartre's play the room felt like hell was because there were no mirrors—even if people wanted to, they had no way to see the reflection of who they were or who they'd become. Sometimes in our desire to protect ourselves, we attempt to remove the mirrors from the rooms we're in by not making it safe for others to tell us the truth. We defend, deflect, or even ignore input from others that just might make our relationships significantly better. It may be tempting to avoid seeing our faults and blemishes; but, as Sartre may suggest, without such insights, we're robbed of the chance to learn and grow.

Can you remember the last time you received feedback? Do you recall the last time you actually asked someone for it? People who take this practice to heart may resonate with Ken Blanchard's quote: "Feedback is the breakfast of champions." I would like to add to it: "Feedback is the breakfast, lunch, *and* dinner of those who know how to build effective relationships." If you recognize that you might *not* be making it safe for others to tell you the truth, let me offer four ways to make it safer:

1. Assume good intent.

Some years ago I was sitting next to my friend and colleague, George, when he stood up to walk to the front of the room to deliver a presentation to a large group of employees. As he stood up, I noticed that his pants had split open. (In this instance, "split" might be an understatement, as the rip would have been akin to describing the Grand Canyon as a minor "split" in the ground.) In George's case, his pants were torn from the waistband to his inseam. Worst of all, he was completely unaware of it! I immediately jumped up and stood behind him to block the audience's view. "Hey, I have a little feedback,"

I whispered. "Your pants are completely ripped out in the back." George froze as I grabbed my sweatshirt from the back of a chair and suggested he tie it around his waist. Fortunately, the dress code was business-casual Friday.

Because this feedback was meant to save George from what could have been a very socially awkward and embarrassing situation, it was easy for him to assume good intent on my part. It's hard to believe someone has bad intent or to argue with an objective statement like "Your pants are ripped," or "You have a piece of spinach in your teeth," especially when you agree with the feedback. However, when the feedback feels more subjective, like "You talk way too much in meetings and shut people down," or "You never share credit with the rest of your team," we become less open to hearing it and more likely to assign bad intent to the person giving the feedback.

As feedback moves from the objective end of the spectrum (you have spinach in your teeth) to the subjective end (you talk too much and shut people down), the more likely we are to interpret it as a personal attack. While he was momentarily embarrassed, George didn't feel threatened. He didn't take my factual feedback as an affront to his character or identity. But when feedback isn't factual, or doesn't jive with our self-perception or experience, it becomes easier to blame the other person as having ulterior motives, to ignore the feedback, or to throw it out entirely.

While you can't guarantee everyone has your best interest in mind, you're far more likely to generate good will and build trust if you assume they do. When you assume good intent, you choose to believe that people are doing the best they can (most people are), and that they sincerely want you to succeed. It means that when you're triggered to shut down or fight back, you instead slow down and get curious about what is being said. Remember, people who have mustered the courage to give you feedback are often feeling as vulnerable sharing it with you as you are receiving it. They are momentarily risking the security of the relationship. When you show up with an open heart, you send a signal that says, "You're safe to share."

2. Ask for feedback.

Assuming good intent makes it safer for you to value others' perspectives; it also gives you more confidence to seek feedback. Successful businesses and organizations do this step frequently. Consider how many times you get an email, a text, or a survey requesting feedback after staying at a hotel or purchasing a product or service. Nearly all large organizations assume their customers and employees want them to get better, so they engage in some type of customer and employee surveying around satisfaction and engagement. Imagine if, as individuals, we had our own customer-service department that followed up and surveyed those we interacted with on a daily basis. I can see it now— your team member/personal customer-service rep asks questions like:

- On a scale of one to ten, how would you rate your recent interaction with Todd?

- What is the primary reason for the score you gave?

- If Todd could do one thing differently to increase your score, what would that be?

- How likely are you to recommend that others interact with Todd?

After getting over the initial shock, consider how helpful that kind of feedback might be. If we make a choice to ask for feedback, others will be far more likely to offer it. But precisely because we don't have customer-service departments working on our behalf, the impetus for requesting feedback is on us.

All of us can benefit from the research that found a powerful correlation between leaders who ask for feedback and their overall effectiveness (defined as their ability to achieve individual goals and objectives).[13] According to the firm Zenger Folkman, the leaders who ranked at the bottom 10 percent in asking for feedback were rated at the 15th percentile in terms of their overall leadership effectiveness. Leaders who ranked at the top 10 percent in asking for feedback were rated, on average, at the 86th percentile in overall leadership effectiveness.

• • •

Recognize that how we ask for feedback can shape the feedback itself and how others choose to give it. One way to discourage people from giving you feedback is surprising them with a request for it. Following a companywide presentation, a vice president came into her team meeting with great enthusiasm announcing she felt her presentation had gone exceptionally well. Others on the team felt that a few key points had been omitted and that the presentation had gone on too long. After she thanked the team for helping her design the presentation, she turned to one of the team members and asked, "So how do you think it went?" In the surprise of the moment, the team member responded, "Great, just great!" While flattered the vice president would ask her opinion, the team member felt unprepared to give feedback, especially in front of everyone. She sensed that her boss really wasn't interested in anything but praise. You could feel the awkwardness in the room, and when the meeting ended, the vice president left convinced the presentation was a rousing success.

So, what went wrong? Sometimes asking, "How did we do?" immediately after an event or assignment isn't the right time. People don't want to be put on the spot and can be especially sensitive to offering feedback that might hurt someone's feelings. In addition, a surprise visit or request is not the ideal way in which to get someone to tell you what you may need to know and hear.

A more effective approach—especially if it's the first time you've asked for feedback—is to let the person know beforehand that you'll be asking for feedback later. Also, a vague question like, "How did I do?" makes it very difficult for people to respond with anything meaningful. A more effective approach would be asking people to share specific things you could do to improve, and to phrase it in terms of behavior or language you might use in the future.

Another way we make it unsafe for others to give feedback is to become defensive when it's given. Kip, a manager and co-worker of mine, once got upset and lost his temper, verbally ripping into a vendor for a mistake they had made. Meredith, another co-worker who had witnessed Kip's angry outburst, approached me and said, "I can't believe someone representing our company in a leadership position would act like that." I shared Meredith's feedback with Kip. He asked for advice on how to handle her complaint. I suggested he write an email and apologize to her. And because I knew Kip well (he tended to be defensive under pressure), I also advised him not to make any excuses for his outbursts—that he admit his behavior was inappropriate and promise not to do it again.

To his credit, Kip immediately wrote the email. And the first paragraph was great: it was sincere, clear, and apologetic. However, in the concluding paragraph, he started to explain and justify why he'd done what he had done. He disregarded the feedback I had given him and launched into a defense of his behavior. His justification both sabotaged his intention with Meredith and also made it more difficult (unsafe) for me to give him feedback in the future. While each of us needs to choose what feedback to pay attention to and what to ignore, we must recognize that rejecting feedback can come at a cost.

Deflecting feedback is another way to make it unsafe. Deflecting is just another version of defending or justifying and sounds something like this: "I hear what you're saying, but I've seen you do the same thing numerous times." People who study such things for a living call this reaction the *ad hominem* (to the man) fallacy. It's so named because of the tendency to ignore the merits of an issue (feedback or otherwise), and instead attack the character of the other person. If you defend yourself or deflect while someone is giving you feedback, you are sending a signal that you're really not interested in feedback at all.

On the other hand, if you ask for feedback in a way that invites only positive feedback (manipulating someone to say only what you want to hear), you're probably not making it safe either. Continually seeking feedback to validate your self-worth isn't the goal. As others pick up on this need, they will either shy away from offering feedback, or be disingenuous because the cost of being truthful is simply too high. In either case, by getting defensive or continually seeking validation, you're not likely to get better.

When you have the courage to ask for feedback with an open

heart and a sincere intent to get better, you'll find yourself. This is exactly what happened to Dana, an employee with great natural talent but not much experience, who started her consulting work with us. After a shaky and less-than-polished first presentation in front of her manager and new clients, she scheduled a meeting with her manager and a more experienced consultant. She asked them if they would be willing to come prepared to share their best practices and feedback on her presentation skills. Ready to take notes with her tablet open on the table, Dana started the meeting, "Okay, I know my first presentation was rough. I have a long way to go. But it's my intention to become as good as you both are. Please give me some specifics on how I can improve and where to start." With each new presentation, Dana had the same follow-up process. She immediately sought out those who were touted as best in class and invited them to give her feedback. It's one thing to ask for a quick opinion at the end of a presentation, but Dana made it a regular practice to engage with different industry professionals for honest input. People who took her up on such invitations had no doubt that she valued their perspective. After many years of soliciting this kind of feedback, Dana is one of our organization's most requested consultants. And while she is excellent at what she does today, she *still* gets better by continuing the practice of making it safe for others to give her feedback.

Listening with a sincere desire to get better will indicate that it's safe for others to tell you the truth. Here's some helpful language when asking for feedback:

"I'm looking for ways to get better at 'x.' Would you consider answering these three questions:

- What am I doing well now?
- What is getting in the way of me getting better?
- Specifically, what can I do differently?"

Sharing feedback isn't always easy, so when people provide it, it's important that we always thank them. As we put our ego aside mitigating the need to be right, we allow our self-confidence to strengthen and our capacities to grow. Thanking them sends a signal that we welcome and will continue to look forward to feedback. I wouldn't hesitate to give Dana feedback, because she's communicated again and again that her sincere intent is to get better.

3. Evaluate the feedback.

If we don't make it safe for others to tell us the truth, not only will we never improve, but we will never get better at deepening our relationships. That doesn't mean we need to act on every piece of feedback that comes our way. It's critical to be clear about the values we stand for (see "Practice 4: Play Your Roles Well") and have a long-term vision of who we want to become so that we are prepared to compare someone's "truth" against what we feel and know is most true for us.

Stephen M. R. Covey knew the expectations that came with being Dr. Covey's son. While he wanted to emulate his father's character and work ethic, he didn't want to be compared to his father when it came to public speaking. Because public speaking had not come naturally and had always been a struggle for him, Stephen M. R. steered his career away from the public eye and toward business administration. But after the publication of *The Speed of Trust*, his own best-selling book, Stephen M. R. was scheduled to attend book-signing tours and speak to large audiences, sometimes alongside his world-renowned father.

At the first event, he walked on stage and delivered what he described as a difficult, intimidating, and mediocre speech as a newly published author. He invited his public relations advisor and a trusted colleague to attend the next speech. During a two-hour meeting following the second event, his colleagues gave Stephen a litany of items to work on. "Be sure to raise the volume of your voice in the beginning to emphasize the first point." "Notice how your father pauses and allows people to think about his phrases. Do more of that." "Make eye contact with everyone, not just the same few people in the audience." "It'll be better if you reorder the speech this way . . ." "Slow down slightly before you end the speech." And the comments went on and on.

Stephen left with no fewer than forty-two pieces of feedback to implement before the next event. He gave it his best shot; but in the end, it backfired. He said that his next speech was the worst he'd ever delivered. Not only were there an overwhelming number of things to focus on, but after reflecting, Stephen realized that many of the suggestions didn't resonate with his natural style. Some didn't align with the approach he knew would best communicate his content. Others were too vague to implement. Even though the ideas might have worked for someone else, they weren't authentic to him or in alignment with who he wanted to become. So he made a strategic decision: He waded through the feedback again; but this time, he chose only those things he felt truly represented who he was and wanted to become. Instead of trying to implement the entire list at once, he chose a few pieces to give his full attention to before the next event and practiced them over and over. Then he chose a few more pieces to work on before the next speech. After many more iterations over the next several months, his ability to deliver effective speeches improved dramatically. He remained open to feedback but was also discerning about what to use and not use. He was able to compare others' feedback against his own truth and determine the best way to up his game in the long run. Now Stephen has become one of the most talented, sought-after public speakers in our company.

We all have moments of insecurity and self-doubt, and receiving feedback can shake even the most confident person. Have a little patience with yourself and be gentle when you feel yourself retreating or wanting to fight back. Remember, in addition to sincerely seeking and evaluating feedback, you can also help people know how to give you feedback. If someone is being vague, such as, "This proposal needs to be stronger," ask for specifics. It might sound like:

- "Will you point out the parts of the proposal that aren't strong enough?"
- "What language might sound stronger?"
- "Can you share with me a sample proposal you like so I can see what you're aiming for?"

And sometimes feedback is not about you. Realize that some feedback—especially when given in angry, reactive ways—is not someone telling the "truth," but rather is someone simply having a bad day and taking it out on you. No one needs to accept verbal abuse disguised as feedback. If someone is angry and harsh with their feedback, you may want to suggest they take a few moments (or hours or days), and return when they aren't feeling so charged.

4. Act on it.

It doesn't do any good to ask for feedback if you have no intention of acting on it. While we don't need to implement every piece of feedback, not acting on feedback—or not explaining why we aren't going to act on it—is worse than not asking for it in the first place. While people may *start to feel* safe when you ask them for feedback, they will *know they are safe* when they see you take their feedback seriously. You help them feel safe by writing the feedback down, demonstrating you are seriously considering what they've shared, and letting them know how you plan to implement what you've learned.

Recognize that acting on feedback can be simple and immediate (like wearing a sweatshirt to cover the split in your pants). But more often than not, implementing feedback takes time. The most entrenched problems we face require a concerted effort to remedy them. Even though feedback might feel like a momentary failure, receive it graciously. And understand that any meaningful change doesn't happen overnight. For instance, in one of Nike's most famous commercials, basketball legend Michael Jordan discusses the topic of failure. He shares that he missed more than nine thousand shots in his career, lost almost three hundred games, and missed the game-winning shot more than twenty-six times. One of the things that set Jordan apart was his mindset of looking at failures as feedback. When he failed to make it onto the varsity team, he returned to the junior squad with an increased desire and focus. His coach would later remark that when he came into the gym each morning at seven, Michael was already there and practicing. This practice continued over the course of the entire year. Regardless of the setback, Jordan carried his own value system and work ethic. He measured himself through the lens of his own standards and accepted feedback as an opportunity to learn and grow. Michael Jordan went on to become the most famous player in the history of the game, winning six NBA championships and five MVP trophies, playing in a dozen All-Star Games, and earning NCAA titles and two Olympic gold medals.

Without exception, the most effective individuals I've worked with are continuously walking the path of self-improvement—making it safe for others to tell them the truth. It was something my friend Meg needed to convey to Carsten, the senior manager at her company, if he was going to understand the importance of asking for feedback . . .

• • •

"It's like he was wearing a T-shirt that said, 'There's nothing you can tell me that I don't already know.' He ignored any of my attempts to give him insight on what he might do better." She sighed.

"Sounds like a difficult coaching challenge for you," I commiserated.

"But here is the worst part," she continued. "The plant was suffering from significant quality-control problems. Ten out of every hundred seals on the tubing kits were defective, and the failure rate was rapidly increasing. The workers were trying to give Carsten feedback on why the error rate was so high, but he didn't want to hear it."

"So, what did you do?" I asked.

"That's just the thing. I didn't do anything!" she replied.

"The failure rate eventually got so high that Carsten knew that unless he solved the problem, he was going to lose his job. Since he'd tried everything he knew, he was essentially forced to start listening to the ideas of others.

"Carsten was having lunch with a fellow manager who happened to mention Lahn, an employee from Vietnam, who had been a regular contributor in team meetings when he was first hired and who had shown great potential in understanding the plant's operations. The manager had told Carsten on more than one occasion how talented and perceptive Lahn was.

"*Carsten later called Lahn into his office and asked him for his advice. During that meeting, Lahn shared an idea he'd been thinking about for quite some time. Carsten was impressed. Together they came up with a way to correct the failure rate. Within a few months, and with continued help from Lahn and others, the failure rates improved remarkably.*"

Meg then shared her subsequent conversations with Carsten. He confided in her that the choice to open up to feedback had made a fundamental impact on him. In Carsten's own words, "*I'm ashamed to admit that my listening skills and being open to feedback were long overdue. I had to take a realistic look at my part of the problem. I needed to get input from the people working on the plant floor who were closer to the problem.*"

Meg said, "*While Lahn's ideas helped solve the immediate quality problem, the whole experience had been a wake-up call for Carsten. Not only did he need to be willing to get feedback, he needed to change the entire feedback systems in the plant to help people feel safe and comfortable coming to management with their ideas. Shortly after that experience, Carsten made giving feedback a fundamental part of every team meeting going forward so that everyone was encouraged to do it.*"

MAKE IT SAFE TO TELL THE TRUTH

Practice making it safe for someone to give you feedback.

---

1. Identify a role you play at work or home that is important to you.

2. Identify at least one person who is influenced by you when you are in that role.

3. Schedule time with that person, asking them to prepare answers to the following questions before you meet:

   - From your perspective, what's working well in our relationship?

   - What isn't working as well or not at all?

   - What, specifically, could I start doing that I'm not doing now to make things better?

4. As they give you feedback, write it down and talk only when you have a clarifying question. Otherwise, listen, listen, listen.

5. Thank them for the feedback in the moment and again later in a note or an email. (Remember, it also takes courage to *give* feedback.)

6. Evaluate the feedback and decide which parts of it you will implement.

ALIGN INPUTS WITH OUTPUTS

DO YOU FIND YOURSELF UNABLE TO CONSISTENTLY GET OR REPLICATE YOUR DESIRED RESULTS?

If so, you may want to consider

PRACTICE 14: ALIGN INPUTS WITH OUTPUTS.

When you don't align inputs with outputs, your room may feel like Sartre's hell because:

- Regardless of how hard you work, your results stay the same—or get worse.
- You begin to doubt and second-guess yourself.
- You see others pass you by.

It's hard not to appreciate stretch jeans—they carry an implicit promise that one can believe the number on the waistband despite how much "stretching" may be required to make it so. It was with this viewpoint in mind that I found myself numbered among the holiday shoppers at a national clothing retailer. My daughter, Alex, happened to be working as a seasonal cashier there, so it gave me the opportunity to drop in and say hello. Her job not only included ringing up and bagging the various items, but handing out brochures and inviting customers to apply for the in-store credit card. I walked over and asked how things were going.

"Okay, I guess," she responded glumly. As a father who had raised several teenagers, I knew there was no such thing as okay—there was joyful and there was miserable, with very little in between.

"What's wrong?" I asked, taking advantage of a momentary lull in the checkout line.

"Nothing, really," she replied.

"Really?" I asked. She knew me well enough to know I had clued in to her apparent frustration.

"Fine. It's just that I get a bonus based on how many people sign up for the in-store credit card, but I don't have many takers." I watched as she rang up the next customer's total and handed them the credit-card brochure. "You can save 10 percent on your purchase today if you apply for our credit card," she announced.

"No thanks," the man responded. After he had paid and left with his items, Alex turned back to me.

"See what I mean?"

"Maybe people are just in a hurry this time of year," I suggested, trying to be helpful. My daughter shook her head and motioned to the next cashier.

"Maybe, except Tiffany's getting a ton of people to sign up. We compared totals on our break and she's killing me. I just don't get why none of my customers want to sign up."

● ● ●

If you happened to be perusing a systems-theory textbook on the topic of inputs and outputs (and who wouldn't?), you'd read that an input is what you put into a system to fuel a process, and an output is the result you obtain. Input, process, output—it's the kind of three-variable system a nonengineering person like myself can get my head around. It's also a useful framework for diagnosing why we get the results we get. To help illustrate what's going on here, let me share a story about urine. (I bet you didn't see that one coming.)

One summer we found burn marks all over the grass at my house. It turned out to be Max's fault (Max is a dog). We bought special green pellets that were supposed to neutralize the acid in Max's system and prevent the burns that destroyed our contribution to the scenic great outdoors. We started Max on the pills and replanted the grass. Imagine our frustration when we found yellow-brown spots on the lawn a few days later. We could have ripped up and replaced the grass every few days, but that seemed a little ridiculous. I could have also replaced my entire lawn with artificial turf, but that came with its own set of problems. Without a plan for moving forward, I simply stood at the window, fixated on the patches of discoloration until it felt like my entire lawn was the color of burned sod. All I wanted was my lawn back in its original, beautiful green condition. I grew more and more annoyed at the whole situation, and even caught myself wondering if maybe it was time for a cat.

During all this plotting over my lawn, I was fixated on the outputs. We can refer to outputs as *lag measures*, or the metrics by which we decide if something is successful. We have all experienced lag measures in our lives: the number on the bathroom scale, the revenue at the end of the quarter, or the report card after the semester. Lag measures show up at the end of a process—by the time they're visible, our ability to influence them has passed. We can get frustrated by them, depressed over them, and even angry at them, but lag measures couldn't care less. I'm certain my lawn was indifferent to the amount of time and energy I spent glaring at it. Spending time and energy to change lag measures is like refusing to leave the stadium after the game is over. Instead, you stare at the scoreboard, steadfast in your resolve that you're not moving until it magically changes and your team is declared the winner.

While it's human nature to get frustrated and focus on the lag measures when things aren't going right, it's best to turn our energy elsewhere. In my own case, instead of dwelling on the outputs around my burned grass, I needed to focus even more on the inputs, or what we call *lead measures*. Lead measures are the actions we take that add up to a lag measure; for instance, the number of doughnuts you eliminate from your daily diet, the quality and quantity of time you spend in face-to-face meetings with your clients, or the evenings you dedicate to homework instead of binge-watching television.

While many inputs might contribute to the desired output, identifying the right inputs can make all the difference. Following are a few examples from FranklinCovey clients who identified the right lead measure from all other inputs they were using to achieve the desired output:

- A health spa found the rate of repeat customers skyrocketed when patrons added thirty minutes to the length of their therapeutic massage session. Right input: The company gives a discount on a ninety-minute session.

- A shoe store discovered that the single biggest factor driving customer loyalty was whether the salesperson measured the customer's feet. Right input: Clerks are trained to offer to measure patrons' feet.

- A national hotel chain realized that when customers checked in under a certain amount of time, they were more likely to be satisfied overall. Right input: Front-desk personnel created a faster check-in process.

So far, I've shared fairly simple examples of connecting inputs and outputs. But the same principle works when tackling large, more complex and systemic problems. Consider New York City in the 1990s. Like many other cities at the time, New York had fallen victim to rampant crime. Midtown's Bryant Park had become an open-air drug market,

Grand Central Terminal a flophouse, and the Port Authority Bus Terminal "a grim gauntlet for bus passengers dodging beggars, drunks, thieves, and destitute drug addicts."[14] Some of the most iconic images of that era are those of the New York subway—dirty, covered in graffiti, and a magnet for crime.

With over 250 felonies committed every week, the New York subway had become the most dangerous mass-transit system in the world. A few insightful people suspected that the city's problems could be traced back to a few lead indicators, such as graffiti. It was argued that such a minor yet visible crime signaled that the government couldn't address the more serious crimes, thereby encouraging more criminal activity. As the mayor at the time remarked, "Obviously, murder and graffiti are two vastly different crimes. But they are part of the same continuum, and a climate that tolerates one is more likely to tolerate the other."[15] An effort was undertaken to aggressively go after lower-level crimes, dubbed the "broken windows" approach to law enforcement. Refocusing their efforts on this input changed everything. New York's violent crimes declined by a whopping 56 percent and property crimes by 65 percent.

Critics argued that the dramatic results had little or nothing to do with broken windows, and the theory remains controversial to this day. But to test aspects of the broken-windows premise, universities began conducting experiments. In one such test in the Netherlands, when an envelope containing five euros was visibly placed in a mailbox, 13 percent of the people who walked past ended up stealing the money. When the same mailbox was covered in graffiti, the number of passersby who took the money doubled to 27 percent![16] The results seemed to validate the focus on graffiti, and low-level crimes were the input that mattered.

People aren't mailboxes or subway cars—we can't just take a bucket of soapy water and scrub away the things that aren't working. But the practice of aligning relationship inputs and outputs has significant merit. This entire book is a series of inputs (fifteen, to be specific) that are designed to help you escape Sartre's hell by building or repairing the relationships you have with those who share your room.

A colleague of mine, Deb, recognized she needed to change a behavioral input with her young son, Dylan. The youngster, who was caught up in the rush of getting out the door and into her car each morning for the ride to school, had a habit of forgetting his shoes. Each morning as Deb was busy getting herself ready for work, she would holler to Dylan, asking if he had everything he needed for the day. On his way to the car, he would dutifully reply that he did. After making the drive to the school, she'd pull up to the curb to drop him off. It was then her son would announce that he'd forgotten his shoes. Frustrated and running late for work, it was natural for Deb to chastise him for not remembering his shoes, even after she'd asked about them. She'd then have to drive back to the house, grab the missing footwear, and deliver her now-tardy child back to the school. This routine happened with enough regularity that my colleague knew she needed to figure out a way to solve the problem for good. Her desired output was to rear a child who was responsible, self-motivated, and in time, fully capable of taking care of himself. With the benefit of hindsight, let me share my colleague's solution to her problem as a five-step process we can all employ:

1. Describe the output you want.

2. Assess the current reality.

3. Examine the inputs.

4. Pick the "lead measure" inputs you think will most likely achieve the desired output.

5. Analyze the result.

The output Deb wanted was straightforward: She needed Dylan to have his shoes on before she drove him to school. The current reality was that he remembered to do it sporadically. The inputs she employed included prompting Dylan to remember his shoes (it didn't work), chastising him for not remembering (to no avail), and racing back home and delivering him late (tardiness means nothing to a seven-year-old). Deb decided to step back and reevaluate her inputs. She wondered if Dylan were to experience the natural consequences of forgetting, it might motivate a change. She decided that instead of returning home to fetch the forgotten shoes, she'd allow him to spend the day in his socks. When the fateful moment arrived and Dylan announced that he'd forgotten his shoes again, his mom didn't turn the car around. "That's okay," she announced. "I guess you'll just need to go to school without them today."

"What? I can't do that!" the boy exclaimed. This outcome was not what Dylan had expected at all. But his mom patiently explained that he could stay inside during recess and that she'd be back to pick him up after school. Unhappy about only wearing socks, the second grader climbed out of the car and made his way to the classroom. Deb finished her commute to work, arriving on time.

The next morning, Dylan remembered to put his shoes on. It was a good start, but my colleague wondered how long it would last. The following day, Dylan remembered his shoes, as well as the morning after that. In fact, the boy never forgot to wear his shoes again! By changing a single input, not only had Deb helped move her son toward the kind of independence she wanted him to achieve, but she saved herself from a ton of anxiety in the process. She discovered how to align the right input with the desired output. Whether helping a child remember to wear his shoes or reducing crime in a large metropolitan city, choosing the right inputs can drive the results we want.

While there are countless inputs that contribute to our relationships, in my experience the fifteen practices in this book are those that have proven to be foundational and of the highest leverage. Implementing even one can be pivotal in repairing a ruptured relationship, restoring trust, and strengthening an already solid relationship. Identifying which of these practices you can use as high-leverage inputs holds the potential to improve even the most stubborn relationship pitfalls.

Let's look back at how each practice can function as an input connected to an important and valued relationship output. While the following table covers inputs and outputs from every practice, reading just a few (or reviewing those that most readily apply to you) will highlight the important difference the right input can make.

Wear Glasses That Work

OLD INPUT	OLD OUTPUT	NEW INPUT	NEW OUTPUT
Todd sees Sydney as someone who needs to be protected and saved.	Sydney gets rescued over and over and never learns to fail and find her own success.	Todd sees Sydney as capable and competent and someone who doesn't need to be fixed.	Sydney becomes a self-sufficient, confident adult.

Carry Your Own Weather

OLD INPUT	OLD OUTPUT	NEW INPUT	NEW OUTPUT
Teacher comes to school every day complaining about what's wrong in the world.	Students learn to blame others or circumstances.	Teacher models that we all have a choice in how to act in any circumstance.	Students learn to take responsibility for their own choices.

Behave Your Way to Credibility

OLD INPUT	OLD OUTPUT	NEW INPUT	NEW OUTPUT
Malee is a very bright woman but is shy and quiet and therefore won't participate or share her opinions in any meetings.	Malee remains stagnant in her role and unhappy that she isn't considered for advancement.	Malee seeks out a mentor in Lisa to help coach her on how to share her thoughts and ideas.	Malee gains confidence and is recognized for her ideas and contributions. One of her ideas saves the company a lot of money and redundancy.

Play Your Roles Well

OLD INPUT	OLD OUTPUT	NEW INPUT	NEW OUTPUT
Rachel is trying to be everything to everybody.	Rachel gets mediocre results in both her personal and professional relationships.	Rachel identifies the most important roles in her life and reorganizes her priorities to spend quality time in those roles.	Rachel has an extraordinary relationship with her daughters while successfully and financially providing for them.

See the Tree, Not Just the Seedling

OLD INPUT	OLD OUTPUT	NEW INPUT	NEW OUTPUT
Rhonda sees only the behaviors that aren't working in her colleague Ava.	Rhonda unintentionally turns co-workers against Ava and limits Ava's potential as well as the relationship with her.	Rhonda starts to identify what Ava does well and starts to see unlimited potential in her.	Ava becomes more confident and starts to succeed in other parts of her job. Rhonda and co-workers begin to believe in her.

Avoid the Pinball Syndrome

OLD INPUT	OLD OUTPUT	NEW INPUT	NEW OUTPUT
Melissa prioritizes urgent tasks over more important relationships.	Garret and other team members feel undervalued and begin to disengage.	Melissa focuses less on urgencies and more on her important key relationships.	Team members feel more engaged and therefore produce higher-quality work that has more meaningful, long-term outcomes.

Think We, Not Me

OLD INPUT	OLD OUTPUT	NEW INPUT	NEW OUTPUT
Lewis takes an independent view: he defines a "win" as him making more money than anyone else on his team.	Lewis is frustrated and jealous when others win, creating a scarcity mentality on his team.	Lewis takes an interdependent view: he defines a "win" when everyone achieves the highest success possible. He views himself winning when everyone else wins too.	Lewis is happier overall, which creates a more abundant culture on his team.

Take Stock of Your Emotional Bank Accounts

OLD INPUT	OLD OUTPUT	NEW INPUT	NEW OUTPUT
Francis creates a withdrawal by blowing up at a colleague. He later apologizes but continues making excuses for his behavior.	Colleague and those around him lose respect for Francis.	Francis focuses on controlling his emotions and making deposits, not withdrawals, in the EBA of others. When he makes a mistake, he apologizes without making excuses.	Francis slowly rebuilds trust with those he's hurt or offended.

Examine Your Real Motives

OLD INPUT	OLD OUTPUT	NEW INPUT	NEW OUTPUT
Sam decides his intentions or motives are to be a leader who invests in building and mentoring his team, but then allows other priorities to pull him off that focus.	Team members feel devalued and not recognized or important.	Sam examines his *real* motives that got in the way of what his healthy intentions were and recommits to put the development of his team first.	Team recognizes Sam's new motives and believes them because of his actions and behaviors.

Talk Less, Listen More

OLD INPUT	OLD OUTPUT	NEW INPUT	NEW OUTPUT
Gary is a talented salesperson, but in his enthusiasm about his product, he does all the talking.	Gary's potential client chooses another vendor who has taken time to understand their problem.	Gary carefully listens first, prior to making any recommendations. Once he listens, he better understands what the client needs.	Client recognizes Gary as a partner vs. a salesperson and values his insightful recommendations.

Get Your Volume Right

OLD INPUT	OLD OUTPUT	NEW INPUT	NEW OUTPUT
Thomas relies only on his perfectionist "go-to" strength and misses the product-launch deadline.	Partners and customers are frustrated when the company's commitments are not met.	Thomas "dials down" his go-to strength when necessary and employs other strengths of collaboration and keeping commitments.	Products launch on time and partners and customers are satisfied. Thomas is perceived as a stronger player and contributor in the organization.

Extend Trust

OLD INPUT	OLD OUTPUT	NEW INPUT	NEW OUTPUT
Rick "leads with suspicion" in most situations, and because he doesn't trust, he requires an inappropriate number of examples, references, verifications, etc.	Rick's company misses many deadlines and beneficial opportunities for partnerships with others.	Rick develops a propensity to trust but with analysis or "Smart Trust."	Projects and associated results led by Rick are of the highest quality, on time, and on budget.

Make It Safe to Tell the Truth

OLD INPUT	OLD OUTPUT	NEW INPUT	NEW OUTPUT
Sam decides his intentions or motives are to be a leader who invests in building and mentoring his team, but then allows other priorities to pull him off that focus.	Team members feel devalued and not recognized or important.	Sam examines his *real* motives that got in the way of what his healthy intentions were and recommits to put the development of his team first.	The team recognizes Sam's new motives and believes them because of his actions and behaviors.

Align Inputs With Outputs

OLD INPUT	OLD OUTPUT	NEW INPUT	NEW OUTPUT
Dylan's mom asks if he has his shoes ready for school before leaving.	As they pull up to drop Dylan off, he announces that he's forgotten to put his shoes on.	Dylan's mom decides to allow her son to experience the natural consequences by going to school wearing only his socks for a day.	Dylan takes responsibility for getting his shoes on every morning.

Start With Humility
(a foreshadowing of the next and final practice)

OLD INPUT	OLD OUTPUT	NEW INPUT	NEW OUTPUT
Talented individual allows his ego and pride to drive him and all of his behaviors. He continually takes credit for everything and makes himself the center of attention.	People talk about him behind his back and strategize how to work around his arrogant, "lone genius" style. Opportunities pass him by.	Talented individual makes a change, sincerely asking others for their feedback. He works on recognizing and acknowledging the contributions of others and stops seeking attention.	Talented individual learns the value of humility and realizes the real satisfaction that comes from collaborating with and focusing on others. Exciting opportunities begin to be presented to him.

Whenever we experience results we're not happy with, there's a strong chance we've misaligned the inputs and outputs. I suspected that was the case with my daughter and her struggle to get customers to sign up for the store's credit-card offer.

• • •

"Maybe people are just in a hurry this time of year," I suggested, trying to be helpful. My daughter shook her head and motioned to the next cashier.

"Maybe, but Tiffany's getting a ton of people to sign up. We compared totals on our break and she's killing me. I just don't get why none of my customers want to sign up."

Alex's predicament had me curious about why the two cashiers were getting such different results. Both kids were average teens getting their first taste of retail work.

"Is she presenting the same card with the same offer?" I asked. Alex nodded yes, looking perplexed.

I walked over to where Tiffany was working. Just as Alex had said, Tiffany was handing the customers the same brochure with the same invita-

tion to save money by applying for the in-store credit card. Then I noticed one small (but as it turned out, significant) input that was different; instead of inviting the customer to save "10 percent," Tiffany was doing the math in her head.

"Would you like to save thirty-one dollars on your purchase today?" she asked. The customer paused, the exact dollar amount seeming to get their attention.

"Yeah, why not?" the customer replied.

I wondered, could that be making the difference? Simply giving the exact total of money saved versus saying "10 percent"?

Walking back to Alex, I said, "I've got an idea for you to try." I explained that rather than using the generic 10 percent language, Tiffany was calculating the savings and sharing the total dollar amount with her customers.

"Oh . . . that makes sense. I guess I'd like to hear what I'd be saving too," Alex replied.

I finished my own shopping and returned to Alex minutes later. Her mood had noticeably improved. As she rang up the total, she leaned forward, "It's working, Dad. I've already had two customers sign up since you left."

A small yet important input. And because I'm probably too accommodating, I ended up applying for the credit card as well.

ALIGN INPUTS WITH OUTPUTS

Identify a current situation or relationship you'd like to improve. Use the template below and the following steps to help align the right inputs with the results you desire.

1. **Describe your desired output in the situation or relationship.** You can't chart a course to a destination if you don't know where it is you want to go. Think of it like a GPS—the more exacting you can be with an address, the more specific it can be in prescribing the route to take.

   I want my team to be energized and engaged about the projects we're working on.

2. **Describe your current reality.** In keeping with the GPS metaphor, we need both a starting point and an ending point to accurately chart a course. Spending time to assess your current reality also helps you uncover potential inputs worth examining and possibly changing.

   Team members come late to meetings and are anxious to leave, very few are enthusiastically volunteering for aspects of the projects, and several side meetings are taking place.

3. **Carefully examine your current inputs.** What things drive the current results you're experiencing? Because inputs are not always intuitive, consider some of the following questions:

   - What paradigms am I holding that might be limiting this person or situation?

   - What am I saying or not saying that could be contributing to this situation?

   - How would the people I work and live with describe my attitude toward them?

- What specific behaviors am I modeling (or not modeling)?
- Would I like me if I were the other person in the situation?

4. **Try a new and more effective input.** Seemingly complex problems can often be dramatically improved by finding the one or two inputs that matter.

5. **Analyze the result.** Everyone fails, but how we consider that failure can make all the difference. As the world-renowned leader and peaceful revolutionary Nelson Mandela said, "I never lose. I either win or I learn." Be objective and thoughtful as you consider the results you're getting, and accept that with each trial and error comes an opportunity to get better.

OLD INPUT	OLD OUTPUT
NEW INPUT	NEW OUTPUT

START WITH HUMILITY

HAS YOUR LACK OF HUMILITY EVER HELD YOU BACK FROM GETTING BETTER? WOULD YOU EVEN KNOW IF IT HAD?

If so, you may want to consider

PRACTICE 15: START WITH HUMILITY.

If you don't start with humility, your room may feel like Sartre's hell because:

- Your ego keeps you continuously looking for external validation that never satisfies.
- You're the topic of side conversations (and not in a good way).
- You miss opportunities to learn because you rarely listen to anybody but yourself.

Now that we're in the final chapter, I have a confession to make. This book wasn't the first I had intended to write. Some years ago I came up with an idea for a leadership book. It was an energizing idea—one for which I had tremendous personal passion. I already began formulating the structure of the book, the narrative flow, and other foundational elements. As I was consumed with putting this work together, the book's title suddenly became clear. I hurried to my computer to purchase the domain in preparation for everything to follow. The topic was humility and, specifically, how the best leaders practice humility in their day-to-day interactions. I wanted to write about people who not only achieved success in their roles but inspired and lifted others along the way, making meaningful impressions on everyone with whom they interacted. With all these ideas in mind, I continued to search for the domain that reflected the exact title of my forthcoming book: Lead With Humility. *When I finished typing and sent my search hurling into the corridors of the internet, what came back stopped me short. I stared at the computer in disbelief—not only was there a book already written called* Lead with Humility, *but it had been written by Pope Francis himself!*

I sat back in my chair and pondered this new development. It looked like I had a decision to make . . .

● ● ●

**"HUMILITY IS LIKE UNDERWEAR; ESSENTIAL,
BUT INDECENT IF IT SHOWS."**

—HELEN NIELSEN, AMERICAN TELEVISION WRITER

Take a moment and consider the most humble person you know. Perhaps it is someone in your family or community, or someone you are currently working with or have worked with in the past, or even someone you've admired from afar. Now think of that person within the context of the fourteen practices outlined so far in this book:

1. **Wear Glasses That Work:** Is their view of the world driven largely by external forces or by an internal compass?

2. **Carry Your Own Weather:** Can they find calm, even in the midst of life's storms?

3. **Behave Your Way to Credibility:** Do they walk their talk?

4. **Play Your Roles Well:** Do they tend to be authentic in what they say and do?

5. **See the Tree, Not Just the Seedling:** Can they see beyond the now?

6. **Avoid the Pinball Syndrome:** Are they good at resisting the temptation of the urgent?

7. **Think We, Not Me:** Do they look for shared wins?

8. **Take Stock of Your Emotional Bank Accounts:** Do they invest in others?

9. **Examine Your Real Motives:** Are they motivated by uplifting rather than diminishing the human condition?

10. **Talk Less, Listen More:** Do they seek first to understand rather than to reply?

11. **Get Your Volume Right:** Do they find appropriate ways to draw upon their strengths?

12. **Extend Trust:** Are they generous and wise when trusting others?

13. **Make It Safe to Tell the Truth:** Do they allow you to feel comfortable being candid and transparent?

14. **Align Inputs With Outputs:** Do their behaviors lead to the outcomes they want?

When I think about the people who have cultivated humility and made it an important part of their lives, it's easy for me to answer *yes* to the majority, if not all, of the questions listed. Above all other character qualities, humility is foundational. It's like salt—it brings out the best flavor of each character quality required for creating effective relationships. The word itself comes from the Latin *humilis*, which literally means "low." But it doesn't express itself as weakness, fear, or timidity. In his book *Humility: An Unlikely Biography of America's Greatest Virtue*, Dr. David Bobb writes that "In reality, humility is strength, not weakness. Humility enables courage and points wisdom in the right direction. It is the backbone of temperance, and it makes love possible."

Those who are humble have a secure sense of self—their validation doesn't come from something external, but is based on their true nature. To be humble means to shed one's ego, because the authentic self is much greater than looking good, needing to have all the answers, or being recognized by one's peers. As a result, those who have cultivated humility as an attribute have far greater energy to devote to others. They go from being consumed with themselves (an inner focus) to looking for ways to contribute and help others (an outer focus). Humility is the key to building solid character and strong, meaningful connections.

So humility *isn't* . . .

- Low self-esteem (thinking you're less than others).
- Low courage (not speaking your mind).
- Ongoing self-deprecation.

Humility is what allows me to say, "I'm sorry. I made a mistake." Humility is what prompts me to think, "What's going on with my co-worker today? Do they need my help?"

Humility is what invites me to step back and make sure everyone in the room receives credit, not just me. Humility is what inspires me to donate my time and resources to a good cause. Humility tells me that no matter how successful I am, I didn't do it on my own. Humility allows me to give my full attention to people when they're talking. It reminds me that *I've* been talking for the last thirty minutes and need to give others air time. Humility helps me feel happy about someone else's success. Humility keeps me curious—in a state of continuous learning. Humility is why I treat the front receptionist with the same respect as I treat the CEO. Humility helps me forgive, even when the person who's wronged me hasn't apologized or asked for forgiveness. Humility tells me there are many right solutions to solving the same problem. Humility invites me to pay it forward. Humility makes me feel grateful for who I am and what I have. Humility prompts me to ask for help when I need it. Humility helps me stop worrying about myself and start thinking about others. Humility allows me to let go of a hurt feeling. Humility gives me courage to be honest with a co-worker in a respectful way. Humility is the wisdom needed to accurately assess my strengths and weaknesses. Humility reminds me to be patient with myself and others, and to know that we are all in the process of getting better. Humility tells me that while I'm important, I'm only one part of a much bigger picture.

"DO YOU WISH TO RISE? BEGIN BY DESCENDING. YOU PLAN A TOWER THAT WILL PIERCE THE CLOUDS? LAY FIRST THE FOUNDATION OF HUMILITY."

—ST. AUGUSTINE

Humility has the power to influence nearly every aspect of your personality. Does that sound like a bit of a stretch? Consider self-control, a trait that is seemingly unrelated to humility. Can humility serve to increase willpower? Researchers conducted a study to answer that very question. They asked a group of volunteers to talk about a time when they felt humble. The researchers listened to their stories, then invited the participants to wait in an adjoining room. It was an ordinary waiting room with couches, chairs, and coffee tables. On each table was a big bowl of candy. By this time, the participants thought they were just waiting for the next part of the study; but the waiting room *was* the next part of the study. The researchers took note of the group's behavior for a time and then dismissed them.

Then they took a second group of participants and asked them to describe a normal day in their lives. When the session ended, the second group was asked to wait in the next room, also supplied with candy. The result: The people who had been asked to describe a time when they were humble ate far fewer pieces of candy! While only 12 percent of the control group abstained from eating candy, 40 percent of the "humble" group ate no candy at all.

After repeating the experiment many times, the researchers came to a remarkable conclusion: People in a humble state of mind are better at self-control.[17] The same set of researchers found that humility can also lead to greater physical stamina and an increased ability to persevere when the going gets tough. And if that's not enough, other researchers went on to find a link between humility and being able to hang on to self-esteem[18] in times of failure, as well as an increased ability to develop stronger social bonds.[19]

As you can see, humility is far from weakness. It allows us to push aside pride, ego, and selfishness while lifting nearly every other important virtue to greater heights.

HUMILITY IN THE WORKPLACE

When talking about work, we rarely use the word humility. It's like people are afraid to talk about it—as if it were the enemy of what it takes to be noticed, promoted, and to succeed. The research, however, says something quite different. According to Professor Mike Austin, Ph.D., professor of philosophy at Eastern Kentucky University, people who are high in humility "lack self-absorption, so they have more courage to try new things. That really frees them up to take risks. . . . They're not paralyzed with a fear of failure because that's not their chief concern." Without failure, innovation stalls. According to Edward D. Hess, Professor of Business Administration at the Darden Graduate School of Business, "Failure is a necessary part of the innovation process because from failure comes learning, iteration, adaptation, and the building of new conceptual and physical models. . . . Almost all innovations are the result of prior learning from failures."[20] To be humble is to be willing to fail in the pursuit of a noble goal. Why does humility express itself in this way? Dr. Austin continues: "Humble people have a habit of thinking about their values when they make choices . . . [They] are more concerned with what is right than being right." Humility allows us to strip away our ego, to suppress the need to be visibly right at every turn, and to take the longer view.

I have known and worked with those who have demonstrated amazing leadership, including someone I'll call Paige, who is the model of humility. More often than not, she has a terrific solution to a problem, but instead of grandstanding or arguing for it, she listens to everyone first and then offers her thoughts. She never refers to a proposed solution as her idea. She actually deflects praise. In one meeting, a colleague asked her, "Tell us about that great idea you mentioned last week."

"Actually, I'd like Randee to tell you about it," she replied. "She's the one who came up with it."

When others are walking out the door at the end of the day, she notices those who are staying to work overtime on a project. More than once I've seen Paige put down her briefcase and call her family. "Hey, I'm going to be just a little late tonight." She rolls up her sleeves and pitches in to help, but she's no pushover.

Like all managers, Paige deals with performance issues on her staff. In another meeting with her, a colleague started playing the victim. He spent fifteen minutes complaining about the extra hours he's put in each day, the personal sacrifices he's made, and how little he is recognized for his efforts. He got increasingly heated as his complaints continued.

To which Paige responded, "I hope you know I appreciate your talents and what you contribute. Frankly, I'm struggling to understand your perspective and what you're saying. Wasn't I just copied on an email from your regional manager outlining how much he appreciated your effort? And haven't I recognized you publicly on several occasions? You've also been in the room when your name came up each time we mentioned the dedicated people we have at the company. So please help me understand what you mean when you say you're not recognized?" It was a perfect balance of courage and consideration, a turning point in the meeting.

This capable, humble leader continues to advance in her career, gaining more and more influence. Ironically, she's the last one you'd see seeking a promotion. Conversely, I've seen people who so badly want influence and control that they end up tripping over their own pride and getting in the way of their own growth and advancement.

There are costs for not putting humility into practice. In a former company, I worked with a very talented man who was continually being passed over for team assignments, projects, and client opportunities he wanted to a be part of for the simple reason that he was too egotistical. His language was often self-referential: "Here's what I did . . ." "I was the first one to land that deal." "I actually started that project." Once, when someone was being recognized for an innovative contribution, he said to a colleague, "So-and-so talks about that as if it were *her* idea, but it was actually mine."

You may have worked with someone like this—the person who is the embodiment of the joke "Well that's enough about me, let's talk about you. What do *you* think of *me*?" When one's ego grows too large or is left unchecked by governors like humility, the price can be huge. In Jim Collins' *Good to Great: Why Some Companies Make the Leap . . . and Others Don't*, he found that "In over two-thirds of comparison cases (average/good companies), we noted the presence of a gargantuan personal ego that contributed to the demise or continued mediocrity of the company." There's little doubt in my mind that such underperforming organizations were ripe with damaged, strained, and broken relationships. When a leader abandons humility, the costs are systemic. Interestingly enough, Collins went on to report that humility was one of the two characteristics he routinely found in leaders who could transform organizations into something great. (The other characteristic was intense professional will.)

I saw a meaningful example of humility in a top sales leader some years ago who received a significant bonus for his amazing revenue results. He called to let me know he appreciated the award, but wanted to see if, through payroll, he could reallocate the money equally among his five team members instead of taking it himself. "I would never have come close to hitting my revenue projection if it hadn't been for those five people," he said. He went on to name each member of his team, detailing how each one had uniquely contributed to the sales process. I replied by letting him know how much I admired his request to recognize his people. But I also explained that because of the written pay plans and legal guidelines, we couldn't reallocate the money he'd earned to his team members. He could, however, gift his team the money after he received his payment.

"But remember, you will have paid taxes on that income before you give it away," I reminded him. He didn't even hesitate.

"Great, I'll do that!"

Don't get me wrong, humility isn't about parting with your money. (If that were the case, Las Vegas might be the humblest city on earth.) It's the attitude of having an outward focus that makes the difference. I also suspect that one of the primary reasons this sales leader's team performed so well was because he made humility a primary attribute when relating to each member. As I've said before, an organization's greatest competitive advantage isn't just its people per se, but the quality of the relationships between them.

Although this is the last chapter of the book, it's titled "Start With Humility" because every practice I've illustrated benefits from obtaining, cultivating, and being mindful of this foundational attribute. And while starting with humility is key, revisiting and recalibrating your humility on a regular basis is equally important. It should accompany every practice, every paradigm, and every moment of thoughtful introspection designed to strengthen our relationships, which is why I'm including the "Get Better" application inside the body of this last practice rather than at the end, to gently but directly invite you to take this practice to heart. While you don't need to complete the application now, read through the instructions and questions that follow. Give each practice some real thought and note how humility influences each one. Then decide when might be the best time to apply it in the upcoming days or weeks.

For the next fourteen weeks, choose one practice to apply. Make
Practice 15: Start With Humility the foundation before you put
any practice into action.

1. Identify a personal or professional relationship that needs attention.

2. Choose one of the fourteen proven practices (described below)
   that you will apply to the relationship.

3. At the start of the week, write down the challenge or opportunity you're experiencing in that relationship. Be as specific
   as you can.

4. Brainstorm how you might apply the chosen practice to the
   relationship, then take careful note each time you interact
   with that person during the week. (What did you think, say,
   or do? How did you feel? What was the impact?)

5. At the end of the week, write about your experience of applying the practice. (What did you learn? Where did you fall
   short? What will you do again next week to get better?)

6. Start the following week with a new practice (and a new relationship or the one you identified originally).

PRACTICE	RELATIONSHIP
Wear Glasses That Work	What belief might you be holding about the person that is limiting the relationship? How might you change it to see him or her more clearly?
Carry Your Own Weather	In what ways are you feeling like a victim in this relationship? What choices do you have to respond differently?
Behave Your Way to Credibility	From the other person's perspective, where do you need to walk your talk? What behaviors do you need to change to be seen as credible in his or her eyes?

Play Your Roles Well	Where have you gotten out of balance in this relationship? What contribution do you want to make in this relationship?
See the Tree, Not Just the Seedling	Have you taken the time to identify what is working, rather than what's not working, in this relationship? What is this person's true potential, and how can you communicate it to him or her?
Avoid the Pinball Syndrome	What one urgent thing can you delay this week in order to address something important to this relationship?
Think We, Not Me	In what ways are you focused only on your win in this relationship? How will you be mindful of everyone's win?
Take Stock of Your Emotional Bank Accounts	How would this person rate the level of trust in your Emotional Bank Account with him or her? What will you do to increase it?
Examine Your Real Motives	Does this person know your true intentions? Have you declared them?
Talk Less, Listen More	Have you taken time to understand this person's perspective on key issues? Are you willing to be influenced by him or her?
Get Your Volume Right	In what ways are you turning the volume up too high on your strengths in this relationship? How will you evaluate and adjust when needed?
Extend Trust	Do you withhold your trust with this person? In what ways might you extend even more trust to him or her?
Make It Safe to Tell the Truth	Have you ever asked this person for his or her feedback about how you're showing up in the relationship? When will you do it?
Align Inputs With Outputs	Have you considered which inputs are contributing to the less-than-ideal results in this relationship? Are you willing to change?

I've used Jean-Paul Sartre's play No Exit as a persistent metaphor and reminder that at the essence of feeling like we're stuck in hell (or conversely, paradise) is our relationships with the people around us. As was noted in the book's introduction, when things become difficult, our tendency as human beings is to find a way out—to head for the exit and move to another room. That might take the form of changing jobs, abandoning associations, or even dissolving marriages and long-standing family ties. These endless "exit strategies" imply that we see external forces (other people and circumstances) as the source of our problems and the means of escape. Yet, we all have the ability to take the focus off the things outside of us (the room and those who occupy it) and move it inward. This internal focus or self-reflection starts with humility. It's the way we begin to get better and strengthen each and every relationship we have.

Now, about the Pope and his preemptive writing of my first book . . . After some reflection, I discovered that Get Better is the book I really wanted to write. And I'm glad I had the wisdom to not compete with His Holiness on the topic of humility by writing a book with the same title. (His book is insightful and inspiring by the way, and I highly recommend you read it.)

When I first saw the title of the Pope's book, I felt like I was too late and should give up and be done. I'm glad I didn't succumb to insecurity. It turns out that fear is an enemy of humility. And when we accept humility into our very core, we find the will to believe more, to do more, and to help others more.

As Sartre wrote, relationships can feel like hell. But on the flip side, if we incorporate these fifteen practices into our lives, relationships can feel like paradise as well. And when it comes to how we spend our brief time on this planet, what can be better than that?

NOTES

1 Sartre, Jean-Paul (1989). *No Exit, and Three Other Plays*. New York: Vintage International.

2 https://www.washingtonpost.com/news/inspired-life/wp/2016/03/02/harvard-researchers-discovered-the-one-thing-everyone-needs-for-happier-healthier-lives/?utm_term=.cb64207aabb8

3 https://rework.withgoogle.com/blog/five-keys-to-a-successful-google-team/

4 Kuhn, Thomas S. (1962). *The Structure of Scientific Revolutions*. Chicago: University of Chicago Press.

5 Frankl, Viktor E. (1984). *Man's Search for Meaning: An Introduction to Logotherapy*. New York: Simon & Schuster.

6 http://mathpages.com/rr/s3-08/3-08.htm

7 https://www.tailstrike.com/291272.htm

8 "Aircraft Accident Report, Eastern Airlines, Inc. L-1011, N310EA, Miami, Florida, December 29, 1972" (PDF). National Transportation Safety Board (report number AAR-73/14). June 14, 1973. Retrieved February 8, 2016.

9 http://www.toyota-global.com/company/toyota_traditions/quality/mar_apr_2006.html

10 Covey, Stephen M. R. (2006). *The Speed of Trust: The One Thing That Changes Everything*. New York: Free Press.

11 Kaplan, Robert E., and Kaiser, Robert B. (2009). "Stop Overdoing Your Strengths." *Harvard Business Review*.

12 Moon, Shawn D., and Sue Dathe-Douglass (2015). *The Ultimate Competitive Advantage: Why Your People Make All the Difference and the 6 Practices You Need to Engage Them*. Dallas: BenBella Books.

13 https://hbr.org/2013/12/overcoming-feedback-phobia-take-the-first-step

14 Manegold, 1992, p.1, as cited in Felson, et al. (1996). "Redesigning Hell: Preventing Crime and Disorder at the Port Authority Bus Terminal."

15 http://www.nber.org/digest/jan03/w9061.html

16 https://www.influenceatwork.com/wp-content/uploads/2012/02/BrokenWindowsArticle.pdf

17 http://www.sciencedirect.com/science/article/pii/S0022103115001183
18 http://psycnet.apa.org/psycinfo/2000-15337-006
19 http://www.tandfonline.com/doi/abs/10.1080/15298868.2011.636509
20 https://www.forbes.com/sites/darden/2012/06/20/creating-an-innovation
    -culture-accepting-failure-is-necessary/#20b0d502754e

INDEX

ABOUT THE AUTHOR

Chief People Officer and Executive Vice President of FranklinCovey

Todd Davis is the author of *Get Better: 15 Proven Practices to Build Effective Relationships at Work*. He is also coauthor of *Talent Unleashed: 3 Leadership Conversations to Ignite the Unlimited Potential in People*.

Davis has more than thirty years of experience in human resources, talent development, executive recruiting, sales, and marketing. He has been with FranklinCovey for more than twenty years and currently serves as chief people officer and executive vice president. He is responsible for FranklinCovey's global talent development in more than forty offices reaching 160 countries.

As the former director of FranklinCovey's Innovations Group, Todd led the development of many of FranklinCovey's core offerings containing the company's world-renowned content, and he continues to contribute to the development of new offerings. Davis has also served as FranklinCovey's director of recruitment and led a team responsible for attracting, hiring, and retaining top talent for the company, which included more than 3,500 employees.

For more than twenty-five years, Davis has delivered numerous keynote addresses and speeches at leading business, industry, and association conferences such as the World Business Forum (WOBI), the *Chief Learning Officer* Symposium, Association for Talent Development (ATD), and HR.com. He has also presented at corporate events and for FranklinCovey clients, many of which are *Fortune*® 100 and 500 companies. His topics include leadership, personal and interpersonal effectiveness, employee engagement, talent management, change management, and building winning cultures.

As a respected global thought leader and expert, Davis has been interviewed by numerous media outlets, including *Fast Company*, *Harvard Business Review*, *Inc.*, and *Thrive Global*.

Davis has served on the Board of Directors for HR.com and is a member of the Association for Talent Development (ATD) and the Society for Human Resource Management (SHRM).

FranklinCovey
ALL ACCESS PASS®

The FranklinCovey All Access Pass provides unlimited access to our best-in-class content and solutions, allowing you to expand your reach, achieve your business objectives, and sustainably impact performance across your organization.

AS A PASSHOLDER, YOU CAN:

- Access FranklinCovey's world-class content, whenever and wherever you need it, including *The 7 Habits of Highly Effective People®: Signature Edition 4.0*, Leading at the *Speed of Trust®*, and *The 5 Choices to Extraordinary Productivity®*.

- Certify your internal facilitators to teach our content, deploy FranklinCovey consultants, or use digital content to reach your learners with the behavior-changing content you require.

- Have access to a certified implementation specialist who will help design impact journeys for behavior change.

- Organize FranklinCovey content around your specific business-related needs.

- Build a common learning experience throughout your entire global organization with our core-content areas, localized into 16 languages.

Join thousands of organizations using the All Access Pass to implement strategy, close operational gaps, increase sales, drive customer loyalty, and improve employee engagement.

To learn more, visit
FRANKLINCOVEY.COM or call **1-888-868-1776**.

FranklinCovey
THE ULTIMATE COMPETITIVE ADVANTAGE

FranklinCovey
THE ULTIMATE COMPETITIVE ADVANTAGE

FranklinCovey is a global, public company specializing in organizational performance improvement. We help organizations and individuals achieve results that require a change in human behavior. Our expertise is in seven areas: leadership, execution, productivity, trust, sales performance, customer loyalty and education. FranklinCovey clients have included 90 percent of the Fortune® 100, more than 75 percent of the Fortune® 500, thousands of small and mid-sized businesses, as well as numerous government entities and educational institutions. FranklinCovey has more than 100 direct and partner offices providing professional services in over 150 countries and territories.

FRANKLINCOVEY
ONLEADERSHIP
WITH
SCOTT MILLER

Join FranklinCovey's executive vice president Scott Miller for weekly interviews of thought leaders, best-selling authors, and world-renowned experts in the areas of organizational culture, leadership development, execution, and personal productivity.

SOME FEATURED INTERVIEWS INCLUDE:

STEPHEN M. R. COVEY
THE SPEED OF TRUST®

KORY KOGON
THE 5 CHOICES®

SUSAN CAIN
THE QUIET REVOLUTION

HYRUM SMITH
PURPOSEFUL RETIREMENT

TODD DAVIS
GET BETTER

DR. DANIEL AMEN
THE BRAIN WARRIOR'S WAY

LIZ WISEMAN
MULTIPLIERS

SUZETTE BLAKEMORE
PROJECT MANAGEMENT

Join the ongoing leadership conversation at
FRANKLINCOVEY.COM/ONLEADERSHIP

SCHEDULE TODD DAVIS
TO SPEAK AT YOUR EVENT

EXECUTIVE VICE PRESIDENT AND
CHIEF PEOPLE OFFICER, FRANKLINCOVEY

Are you planning an event for your organization? Schedule Todd to deliver an engaging keynote speech, tailor-made for today's leaders at events like these:

- Association and Industry Conferences
- Sales Conferences
- Executive and Board Retreats

- Annual Meetings
- Company Functions
- Onsite Consulting
- Client Engagements

Schedule today by calling 1-888-554-1776 or visit **www.getbetterbook.com**